HOW TO BUY & SELL CRYPTOCURRENCIES BITCOIN, ETHEREUM AND ALTCOINS 2022

CRYPTOCURRENCY INVESTMENT STRATEGIES
TO IMPROVE YOUR BUSINESS

CONTENTS

DISCLAIMER

earnings, exact earnings or promises for actual or future performance.

INTRODUCTION

Interest rates being offered for savings accounts are at record low levels. Bonds and treasury notes are barely keeping up with the rate of inflation. The stock market is showing signs of slowing down. The cost of goods and services is rising as the government prints and pumps more money into the economy. It's becoming more of a challenge to grow one's wealth under these current economic conditions.

You shouldn't blame yourself, the government, your employer or anyone else for that matter as to what is transpiring. Complaining is not going to solve the current financial hardships or realities you're faced with right now. You can whine and complain all you want. It's not going to change your present reality. The current reality is that as long as governments keep printing money at will, your purchasing power will diminish.

Now, it's time for action. Imagine not having any financial worries, being in the enviable position of providing yourself and your loved ones with the lifestyle you've been dreaming about. Imagine not having to rely on the government to pay for your desired lifestyle, free to enjoy life on your terms. No longer would you have to rely on someone else dictating what your future will hold and when you can retire. You would be in control, with little or no financial worries.

What you're about to explore in this book is a means to be able to rise up from your current financial situation and embrace a new exciting reality. A reality of hope and optimism. All brought about by a little-known asset class called cryptocurrencies. You're about to discover how to tap into the incredible wealth generation potential of this new asset class.

Unfortunately, a lot of cryptocurrency books in the marketplace share one common element with each other, they do not provide detailed step-by-step instructions as to how to invest in this new asset class based on current best practices. What was solid investment advice in 2019, is no longer applicable in today's landscape. That's about to change with this guide.

The insights and strategies being shared in this resource are life changing. By the end of this guide, you will:

- have a much clearer understanding of how to invest in cryptocurrencies from the perspective of a novice and intermediate investor.
- learn new investment strategies that capitalize on crypto investing in a bigger way in the upcoming years.
- gain confidence in investing in cryptocurrencies.
- create more clarity in your overall investment plan.

You may be hesitant about investing in this new asset class. That's understandable. There are several common myths in circulation that are holding back many potential investors. One of the biggest is that it's too late to get into the crypto market; that you've missed all of the big gains.

It is true that depending on when you enter the cryptocurrency market, you may have missed out on the huge gains that can often be attributed to a massive upswing in coin prices during a bull market. However, a deeper look at how this market is evolving has shown that the annual rate of return for the predominant coin - Bitcoin - has been just shy of 230 percent per annum over the past decade. In comparison, the S&P 500, a popular stock market index has returned about 12 percent per year over the same period.

Even if Bitcoin or another popular crypto only generated a 40 or 50 percent return on average when held long-term, most investors would be ecstatic. Who wouldn't want to potentially quadruple their money in less than ten years? I would be stoked at the prospect of receiving an even lower double-digit return, knowing what most other markets are capable of generating as far as average annual returns.

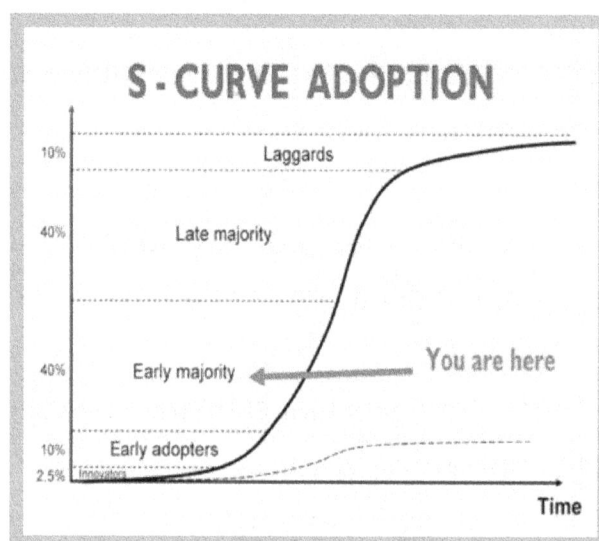

Another prevalent myth you may have come across is that you need to be tech savvy or have previous trading skills in other asset classes in order to invest in cryptos. It does help to have an inkling as to how to use a smart phone and be comfortable with online transactions; however, even if you're a complete newbie you can gradually acquire the skills necessary in order to use any blockchain network.

It's not necessary to fully understand how the technology works beyond the key insights you need to invest in opportunities. Much of the focus of this guide is to close the gap between what you should know and what your current level of understanding is. Once you understand the key concepts associated with this new technology, you'll be in a better position to make sound investment decisions.

And finally, I've saved the juiciest myth for last that the crypto market is ultra-risky. It's a market that experiences wild price swings and you could potentially lose all of your money overnight. Yes, this is a possibility. Given the 10-year track record for the most popular cryptocurrencies in the marketplace, this scenario is becoming less likely to occur.

This is best described by Metcalfe's Law, which holds that as the number of users grows linearly, the network's value grows geometrically. In other words, Bitcoin's value should grow faster than does its network of buyers, sellers, exchanges and participating retailers. A recent example of this phenomena is with worldwide mobile phone subscribers where market growth was not linear over the past two decades but exponential. Bitcoin is following a similar pattern of exponential growth in value.

In fact, Galaxy Investment Partners CEO, Mike Novogratz in a March 6, 2021 interview said:

> "Cryptos have experienced a paradigm shift. It became a new institutional asset class in 2021."

This means that more institutional investors will embrace cryptocurrencies as an asset to hold in their massive portfolios.

As with any new market experiencing growing pains, cryptocurrencies have had their wild swings in the past from having gains well in excess of 100 percent to losing 70 to 90 percent of their values. Much of the excessive volatility experienced in the early years is being worked out of the system. As the overall market gains in popularity, those wild price swings will also diminish.

And should you decide to hang onto your initial positions for the long haul, time will reward you handsomely down the road. This is because demand for Bitcoin is growing exponentially while the supply approaches its limit of 21 million coins. Bitcoin is acting as a store of value because of its scarcity.

True, the current massive gains and losses in the market are unnerving but once you understand the growth potential of blockchain technology and those coins supporting the networks, you'll begin to fully appreciate the fact that you're at the right place at the right time.

So, who's this particular guide for?

First off, this book doesn't go in-depth into the history of cryptocurrencies and common information that can be found on the Internet. There are plenty of resources available that focus on just that. What this guide does do is it provides you with a brief overview of those key concepts and terminology needed to fully understand the investment process particular to cryptocurrencies.

This guide is divided into two sections to address the needs of both the novice and intermediate investor. For the novice investor chapters 1 to 7 set the stage as to:

- How to build your investment portfolio.
- How to set up secure accounts before buying cryptos.
- How to select an appropriate crypto exchange that'll meet your current and future needs.
- How to protect your holdings with wallets.
- And how to buy cryptos on an exchange or through a peer-to-peer transaction.

The second part of this guide delves deeper into the world of crypto investing. In chapter 8 to 13, the intermediate investor will learn more about:

- Those factors affecting a coin's price.
- How to assess potential investment opportunities for Altcoins and tokens.
- How to use several entry strategies for buying cryptos.
- How to optimize your long-term returns.
- And what tax implications you should be aware of.

The focus of this guide is to empower you with a deep understanding of the investment process unique to cryptocurrencies from setting up various accounts and tools to determining which cryptos offer the greatest growth potential and how to enter and exit the market with a high probability of generating a positive return.

If you're a novice crypto investor this guide will literally take you by the hand and explain step-by-step how to set up the various accounts, platforms and tools you'll need in order to become a successful long-term investor. You'll have a good understanding of how cryptos are priced in the marketplace and how to safely enter and exit positions. I'll be sharing many insights into how to build sustainable long-term wealth while avoiding many of the pitfalls of investing.

If you're already dabbling in the odd cryptocurrency acquisition, then this guide will take you from where you're at, to where you might want to take your investing down the road. You'll be able to tap into a myriad of proven investment strategies. For those who would like to take on a more active role in the investment process, then this guide shows you how to assess potential plays and incorporate various market timing strategies.

I've always believed that real learning doesn't take place until it changes your behavior. This guide is set up with actionable steps you can take that'll bring you closer to creating greater financial freedom in the pursuit of your desired lifestyle.

My passion for investing spans over three decades in various marketplaces. Having written a half dozen books already in the investment niche, I hope that this particular guide will empower you to reach a point of financial freedom sooner.

Ready to embark on a journey of discovery into the world of cryptocurrency investing?

~

WHY CRYPTOCURRENCIES?

This chapter will provide you with an understanding of how cryptocurrencies came into existence along with some of the key concepts and terminology you should be familiar with before investing. The primary focus of this chapter is to shed some light on how blockchain technology is shaping the way we operate in an ever-increasing digital world. Once you have a solid understanding as to how the cryptocurrency space is set up, we can explore the risks and rewards of crypto investing in the following chapter.

The Rise of Bitcoin.

The concept of creating a digital currency is not new. Digital cash was being used in the 1980's. Digicash was the first digital payment system that used a digital currency called cyberbucks to make online purchases. Designed for small online retail purchases, users converted their bank money into Cyberbucks in order to make purchases. Unfortunately, Digicash was not much different from credit card technology and the company filed for bankruptcy in 1998.

In 2008 along came Bitcoin. A person or group calling themselves Satoshi Nakamoto published the white paper: "Bitcoin: A Peer-to-Peer Electronic Cash System", which rocked the computer science world. The paper arrived soon after the 2008 stock market crash. It described how an electronic payment system could be implemented based on cryptographic proof instead of trust in government or public financial institutions. This ended up being perfect timing as it provided an alternative financial instrument to fiat currencies.

In September 2009, the first exchange listed 1309 Bitcoin for sale for $1. Fast forward to 2021 and those Bitcoin would have a street value of over $66 million. As Sponge Bob Square Pants says: "That's impressive all right". When someone offers you a seat on a rocket to the international space station, you don't ask where you'll be sitting. You just get on and go for an exciting ride. And this is what the cryptocurrency world is doing right now.

During the 2008/ 2009 recession, the US federal government pumped money into the market to create liquidity. This practice is known as quantitative easing. It led to a devaluation of the US dollar and other fiat currencies worldwide. The purchasing power of a fiat currency diminished, resulting in the cost for goods and services to increase. By the way, the term "fiat currency" refers to the value attributed to a currency based solely on a government decreeing it to be so. Most countries use fiat currency issued by a central bank as a means of legal tender. This means that the government controls the supply and that affects its value.

As a general rule of thumb, the more fiat currency that is printed, the greater the level of devaluation of the existing supply, which results in a rise in the rate of inflation. To combat this, most central banks lower interest rates making it easier for financial institutions and consumers to better cope with an inflationary environment. The country's central bank can boost the liquidity of the economy as it sees fit.

A slight rise in the rate of Inflation is positive when it boosts consumer demand and consumption that drives economic growth. Although most economists feel that increasing the money supply during severe recessionary periods helps the overall economy, it does pose some additional problems. Too much money entering the overall market erodes your purchasing power and can lead to the hyper-inflation of the currency whereby consumers experience a shortage of goods as prices rocket skyward.

Bitcoin is the most popular decentralized cryptocurrency in the world. And what do I mean by "decentralized"? No single institution controls the coin's existence. It relies on no one bank, government or middleman to operate. Nor can anyone change any information or make sweeping policy changes. It is a true peer-to-peer network in which each person acts as both an owner and user.

You could compare the decentralization process to how major search engines on the Internet operate. Millions use these search engines at the same time, yet the system doesn't slow down. This is because the search engines run on many separate servers worldwide making it nearly impossible to bring down the entire network. Cryptocurrencies spread out the functions relating to the control, accounting and production of the digital currency across multiple "nodes". Which brings us to the question ...

What is Blockchain Technology?

Blockchain technology is comprised of two basic parts:

- a "block" of digital information and
- a public database called the "chain" that stores the information.

Each blockchain has a time stamp and is linked to the previous block through a "hash" code making it a chronological event. The information is batched or "blocked" together so that one block references the one prior to it. This creates a "chain" of transactions. For Bitcoin, Satoshi Nakamoto used open-sourced blockchain code so that anyone can use the code, make improvements, or build entirely new platforms based on this basic code.

Fortune Business Insights estimates that the blockchain market will grow by a staggering 56.1 percent every year until 2027 reaching a market cap of $69.04 billion. This means that investment opportunities will not only exist in specific cryptocurrencies but also the platforms and businesses that are built around the blockchain technology. And many of these upcoming businesses will be listed on various stock markets thus expanding your investment options down the road.

What is unique about this technology is that everyone in the blockchain network can get a copy of the whole database, should they so desire. The network uses an open ledger format that can be viewed anytime by any individual worldwide who would like to watch transactions taking place in real time. This makes it extremely difficult to manipulate, if not impossible, since multiple sources can trace the flow of transactions occurring.

An Ocean of Opportunity:

The crypto community likens the crypto market to the ocean, which is teaming full of big and small fish or users. Often a crypto rally is referred to as a "feeding frenzy", with "waves" being market movement. Much of the terminology surrounding the market has its roots in this "ocean of investors" metaphor.

The term "whales" refers to the big players and institutions like Hedge Funds and Crypto Investment Funds. For example, whales make up approximately 1/3 of all Bitcoin investors in the market today. These groups have the collective power to move the markets creating buy/sell trends within a specific market. Some of the well-known funds that hold cryptocurrency positions are:

- Pantera Capital
- Bitcoins Reserve
- Binary Financial
- Coin Capital Partners
- Falcon Global Capital
- Fortress
- Bitcoin Investment Trust
- Global Advisors Bitcoin Investment Fund

to name a few.

There are a few terms you should be familiar with as you explore the exciting world of cryptocurrency investing. You'll often hear the term "hodl" or "hodling", which refers to holding onto your coins and tokens long-term. You'll also come across the term "sats", which is short for "satoshis", a term used to describe the smallest fraction of a Bitcoin that can be sent. In the world of Ethereum the smallest Ether coin fraction is known as a "gwei".

You'll also come across the term "gas" fees, which refers to the transaction fees you incur when you buy and sell cryptos on the Ethereum platform. These are the fees that the miners receive from users to compensate for the computing energy required to process and validate transactions on the blockchain. These fees are not unique to Ethereum, all other cryptocurrency networks compensate their miners for maintaining the blockchains involved.

And the term "pump and dump" is used to describe buying and selling coins and tokens. When something is "mooning" it refers to a coin or token spiking in price. No. it doesn't refer to pulling your pants down to your ankles in public.

The Arrival of Altcoins

Soon after the arrival of Bitcoin, programmers and developers launched the first alternative digital coins into the marketplace in 2011. These alternative digital currencies became known as Altcoins. There are currently thousands of Altcoins in the digital currency marketplace of which the most popular is the Ether coin supported on the Ethereum blockchain network.

Vitalik Buterin, a Russian Canadian programmer, created the Ethereum decentralized software development platform back in 2013. Public sale of Ether started in July 2014 with an "initial coin offering" or ICO price of $0.40. In the six years since its inception, Ether has climbed to over $2000. And this may only be the beginning.

Developers and programmers can use the Ethereum code to build blockchain based applications. Ethereum is built around "smart contracts", which are self-executing terms and conditions. Smart contracts are based on the notion of having a set of conditional (if - then) statements followed by a specific action. For example, IF I pay my landlord $1500 at the beginning of the month, THEN I can use the apartment to live in.

Smart contracts take care of all aspects of a transaction:

- management,
- enforcement,
- performance, and
- payment.

Smart contracts are also:

- self-executing,

- letter strict,
- immutable (can't be changed) and
- secure.

Since the Ethereum platform is open source, anyone can launch a "decentralized application" or DAPP. These are apps that do not require a central authorizer like Google to function. Programmers and developers have already launched over 1500 different DAPPs across a multitude of industries based on the concept of using smart contracts. This includes applications for games, finances, exchanges, personal identification, health, and property. By unlocking the potential of blockchain technology, Ethereum has become the second largest cryptocurrency in terms of market cap.

The term "nodes" refers to the "miners" who are the individuals or collectives running the computers that run the Ethereum platform. And the cryptocurrency used to incentivize users to run the Ethereum model on their computers is called Ether. Whereas Bitcoin is described as being "digital gold", Ether is more like "digital oil". It fuels the Ethereum network.

The major difference between Bitcoin and Ether is that Bitcoin has a fixed supply of 21 million coins, which need to be mined over time to integrate into the network. A cap on the number of coins has the advantage of making the crypto inflation proof. On the other hand, Ether's supply has not been permanently capped at a fixed level. It may or may not change the number of available coins in the future.

Since both the Bitcoin and Ethereum networks are open-sourced code platforms, no one person can change the protocols set up. It requires the consensus of a majority of programmers and developers to make changes to the coding. With Bitcoin, developers can submit a "Bitcoin Improvement Proposal" or BIP, which is essentially a document that proposes the changes to the core Bitcoin technology. For example, in 2012 and 2015 two major changes came about for the Bitcoin platform with BIP-9 and BIP-34. The number following the BIP acronym refers to the unique proposal being considered.

On the Ethereum network, developers submit an "Ethereum Request for Comments" or ERC. For example, ERC-20 was a proposal for the establishment of rules governing the use of tokens on the Ethereum blockchain network. Currently, there are over 1/4 million different tokens being used on the network as a form of digital payment. Some of the more popular tokens are Tether, Chainlink, Vchain and BAT (basic attention form).

Which brings us to the notion of tokens, what they are and why you should take notice from an investment perspective.

What are non-fungible tokens?

When we attribute objective value to an asset, someone's beliefs, attitudes or perceptions do not affect the value of the entity. The value is inherently derived from the asset itself. It's not based on a subjective opinion. For example, no one would argue that a glass of water in the desert doesn't have a functional value. Whereas the value of a bus ticket to Winnipeg, Manitoba in January depends on whether or not the individual wants to go to Winnipeg or not in the time frame stipulated on the ticket.

We can see from the above context that an asset is something useful or valuable. It can be in a physical form like gold, a digital form like Bitcoin, an intellectual or abstract form like professional expertise and in a financial instrument form like a 401K investment account.

A "fungible" asset is one that can be swapped with another asset of the same type. Fungible assets like a $50 bill or a Bitcoin are interchangeable. The value doesn't change between them.

A "non-fungible" asset is one that is not interchangeable or divisible. For example, two houses do not represent the exact same value exchange. It's not an equal swap of value, since each house is in a different location, has a different yard and comes with a unique history of ownership.

Tokens are something physical or digital that can be exchanged for or represent a good, a service or another form of value or utility. In the cryptocurrency world tokens are used for representing a:

- stake,
- toll,
- currency,

- voting right,
- store of value,
- ownership, or
- multifunctional application.

A token doesn't have value in and of itself. It has value based on the asset it represents. Tokenization is the process of creating a token that has an associated asset attributed to it. Tokenization in the crypto world uses blockchain technology to store decentralized data that is unmodifiable and exists in a global transparent network or environment.

A "non-fungible token" or NFT is a digital representation of a unique asset that can be equally swapped or traded with another NFT of the same type. NFT's can represent a host of items like digital art, a ticket to an event, virtual property or even a deed to a physical piece of property.

Block chain technology through NFTs provides ownership, management permissions, and transferability. All of this occurs on a decentralized, transparent and immutable platform. For example, Opensea.io is a peer-to-peer NFT marketplace where you can purchase, sell, trade and exchange non-fungible tokens. The website has numerous categories for art, domain names, virtual worlds, collectables and trading cards.

Six key properties inherent with NFTs that'll shed some light on how blockchain technology and tokenization are changing the way in which we conduct transactions are:

1. Standardization

Traditional digital assets currently don't have a single platform that they can all exist on. For example, electronic tickets reside on Ticket Master's platform, while Fortnite character skins reside on Fortnite's platform. These are separate places where their digital assets exist. By tokenizing these types of digital assets on the blockchain, users can create NFT's with set standards and uniformity. All of the aspects of NFT's like ownership, transfers, access and control are unified on one common system.

Imagine if you purchased a digital house on one site along with some digital artwork on another. Developers using the same decentralized platform, like Ethereum, could build applications using the same code that would allow you to be able to place the artwork inside of the house.

Setting standards and uniformity across platforms through NFTs is paving the way for highly complex real-world applications. From an investment point of view, advances in smart contract applications will change how entire industries will operate in the future. Being aware of these technological changes is just the first step in the awareness process of identifying potential investment opportunities.

2. Interoperability

This property just means that NFTs created on a network like Ethereum use the same standards. This allows NFTs to move easily across multiple ecosystems. When a developer creates a new NFT, it becomes immediately viewable and tradeable on all NFT marketplaces, in virtual worlds and other applications due to the standardization of the data being recorded on the network's blockchain.

3. Tradability

Interoperability allows for free trade on open markets. NFTs can instantly be displayed on marketplaces across the entire ecosystem. In these various marketplaces, users can buy, sell, trade, exchange, bid, bundle and auction off NFTs for cryptocurrency. This allows us to transcend from a centralized buying hub like eBay or Amazon to a decentralized, true, open, free-market economy. The ease with which people can create, launch and trade NFTs across the entire blockchain ecosystem will revolutionize the game development industry since virtually everyone will be able to contribute creative content to the games. It won't be up to the initial game developers to improve the gaming experience.

4. Liquidity

When you have fast, efficient tradability on marketplaces you also create high liquidity at the same time. More people are able to buy and sell in the marketplace at a faster frequency with lower price volatility. Items bought and sold won't experience dramatic fluctuations in price or wild price swings seen in rarely used marketplaces with low transaction volumes. Bitcoin is a good example of a marketplace that experiences high transaction volume and liquidity. There are a lot of buyers and sellers, so transactions occur almost instantly. Contrast this with buying and selling a house. Once you put your house up for sale, it may take weeks or months to find a buyer. This market has a low liquidity rating compared to currency exchanges.

5. Immutability

Immutability is a key pillar of blockchain technology. Any data that has been verified and recorded to a blockchain ledger cannot be changed. This provides holders of NFTs a way of ensuring the authenticity of any digital asset and can be used to prove its scarcity. For example, imagine your $5000 eBike gets stolen and you see it three doors down in the neighbor's garage. How do you prove it's yours? If you have a smart contract token proving current ownership, this solves the problem. If you decide to sell your eBike, you transfer the current ownership through the token. This type of smart contract application will radically change how we conduct business in the future.

6. Programmability

The final property that blockchain brings to the table that makes NFTs so valuable is programmability. Non-fungible tokens are fully programmable thus allowing immense complexity like redeeming, random generation, forging and crafting.

Non-fungible tokens are currently being used in art, gaming, collectibles, virtual worlds and domains. When you take into account NFT's six core properties, these tokens can be used in a myriad of future industries. For example, musicians and filmmakers could register their work on a blockchain in the form of an NFT to protect it from copyright infringement and manage performance rights. This would remove the need for intermediaries like agents and managers. One hundred percent of any funds generated could go directly to the rightful creators of the content without third party intervention.

Since NFTs are completely programmable, people can create non-fungible tokens that contain cryptocurrencies and digital files. These NFTs can be traded and redeemable for real world assets like vehicles, real estate, clothing items, household goods, electronics and recreational equipment. All of these items could be redeemed for the item in question, traded on the open market, held while the price appreciates or sold when you're ready.

Virtually anything in the real world can be tokenized. NFTs could also represent official documentation like birth certificates, government-issued photo identification, academic credentials, medical records, warranties, DNA data, etc. The possibilities are endless. And NFTs will radically change how we interact with each other in the future. No longer will you need to have middlemen like:

- Notaries to handle real estate sales.
- Insurance companies to handle medical claims with hospitals.
- Escrow agents to handle financial transactions between parties.
- Banks to handle international currency transactions.

- Brokers to handle stock purchases.

Replacing third party involvement for many real-world applications will reduce overall costs, increase transaction speeds and eliminate many restrictive barriers already in place. Non-fungible tokens are going to introduce new people to the cryptocurrency market and drive adoption of blockchain technology. For this reason, it's important to understand how these current developments and trends are going to impact society down the road.

Granted these changes will not happen overnight. Building decentralized applications for NFTs is time consuming and challenging. And many of the current NFT projects don't currently have a lot of users, which means that there is a lack of liquidity that's stifling growth. However, once technology has more time to develop, we'll begin to see a lot more progress and growth in the space, along with investment opportunities for you.

As well, user experience with the concept of NFTs and user interface with the technology are in their infancy. There simply aren't enough people familiar with blockchain applications for solving common industry problems to see a wholesale shift in how these industries will operate in the future. Many will resist the obvious beneficial and welcome changes because the jobs of the middlemen will become obsolete.

Now that you have an idea as to how non-fungible tokens work, this should give you a better perspective about the future of tokens. What's encouraging is that you're super early to the NFT party as many of the guests have yet to arrive on the scene. As token popularity catches on, so too will investment opportunities in those tokens that offer unique applications. And as industries embrace blockchain technology more options for investing will open up. Not only will some cryptocurrencies experience rapid growth, but businesses built on blockchain networks will also benefit from radical changes occurring in those industries.

Now that you have a better understanding as to how blockchain technology is evolving, it's important to keep your eye open for those opportunities in both the cryptocurrency and equity marketplaces. Each market can provide you with unique investments that'll help you grow your capital over time while diversifying your exposure in the crypto space.

It's also important to learn how to assess those opportunities that have a high probability of success. You're looking for sustainable growth of whatever asset you're holding. We'll address these aspects later in this guide. Now, it's time to look at the risks and rewards that this asset class can present.

~

THE RISKS AND REWARDS OF CRYPTOCURRENCIES

One of the most important questions any investor in the cryptocurrency marketplace needs to answer before investing is: Why should I trust cryptocurrencies?

In order to arrive at this decision, it would be helpful to explore the pros and the cons of investing in this relatively new asset class. Once you understand the nature of any potential risks and weigh those against the potential rewards, you'll be in be in a better position to assess whether or not cryptos are for you. Even if you never purchase a coin moving forward, you'll at least have expanded your financial IQ and your understanding of this new asset class.

Potential Risks:

Some of the biggest obstacles or challenges the cryptocurrency market is experiencing right now can be placed into 10 different potential risk categories, as follows:

1. Decentralized Status: No backing by a centralized authority.

Most markets are controlled by a centralized authority, usually a government-sponsored agency. Being centralized, you have a sounding board to turn to when problems arise. We're used to dealing with financial institutions who are governed by strict rules of conduct making the resolution process more predictable for the average consumer.

By far the vast majority of cryptocurrencies operate on decentralized platforms, making them more challenging to operate in when transactions don't work out as planned. When legal complications arise with transactions, there is no regulated financial institution behind the transactions taking place. You don't have a government agency or institution you can go to for help with your issue. This means that you're on your own as an investor when moving into and out of the crypto market. Fortunately, you do have this guide and other online educational resources you can reference in order to make any process as seamless and straight-forward as possible.

2. Lack of extensive regulation of exchange platforms.

It's the Wild West right now in the crypto space as exchanges offering to buy and sell cryptos come under stricter regulatory control. Unlike the banking sector, which adheres to many government guidelines requiring the financial institution to "Know Your Customer", crypto exchanges vary greatly in how client information is gathered and stored. Currently, strictly digital payment systems are not universally regulated the same as financial institutions offering fiat currency payment options. This is slowly changing as more and more national governments begin regulating the industry.

3. Fraud and money laundering.

Criminal organizations currently use digital currencies for these purposes. Money laundering happens on an international scale with all fiat-backed currencies. It's no different for cryptos. What was alarming, were the number of early exchanges who were hacked and cryptos were stolen never to be recovered. The most famous hack occurred at the Mt Gox exchange in Japan in February 2014. This exchange alone was responsible for 70 percent of global Bitcoin transactions at the time. After suspending trading, the exchange became insolvent having lost about 7000 Bitcoins in the hack attacks. This reality is a serious concern for any investor. News of security breaches at crypto exchanges can impact user confidence of the cryptocurrency market as a whole. Although it's currently a rare occurrence in 2021, it can have an immediate impact on the value of many coins.

4. High volatility compared to other markets like the stock market.

Wide price swings can make cryptos a risky form of investment in the short term. As with any new market experiencing growing pains, you'll see large fluctuations in the price with traders, as opposed to investors, being the major market movers. Mainstream investment firms have been slow to commit large portions of their cash to cryptos. However, this changed in 2021 as more hedge funds and major corporations have allocated a portion of their capital to longer term cryptocurrency investments. Over the next few years, expect to see high market volatility until main street adoption by large financial institutions, who are investing in cryptos for the long-term, play a significant role in mitigating the market volatility.

5. Inadequate user support for many Altcoins.

The fewer the number of players, the more dramatic the price fluctuations can be. This is especially so with new start up currencies that may see their coins or tokens lose value if there isn't an adequate number of users. Being such a new market with few buyers and sellers, certain cryptos can be subject to wide price swings. Just a handful of users can move the market significantly with some of the smaller cryptos. When you contrast this to the stock market with its millions of users, wild price swings are much less frequent compared to the crypto space.

6. Lack of support from world economies.

Some countries like Algeria, Bolivia, Bangladesh, Saudi Arabia and Vietnam have outright banned cryptocurrencies. Others like India, China, Ecuador, Indonesia and Egypt do not fully support cryptocurrencies, having imposed restrictions. As of 2021, most popular financial institutions are opposed to cryptos. This lack of support and confidence in the crypto marketplace makes it challenging for citizens, entrepreneurs and investors alike. Even as I write this guide, countries are coming out for and against cryptos. Cryptos are experiencing challenges to being adopted worldwide.

7. Negative influence of the press.

Any news that a central government is considering regulating cryptos can create fear amongst users and disrupt the market's value. Bad press can cause a crypto to plummet in value. The worst type of news affecting cryptos relates to the outright ban of cryptos or their treatment under security laws. News related to combatting money laundering or the financing of terrorism also has a negative effect but to a lesser degree. Fortunately, the more well-established cryptos, with an active user base, have often quickly rebounded back after the effect of bad press has worn off.

8. Slow worldwide adoption.

The cryptocurrency market is a relatively new asset class that's slowly developing worldwide. Much attention to cryptos has been given to the North American consumer market in 2020. However, the understanding and adoptions of cryptocurrencies as an exchange of value is slow in coming. Only an estimated 20 million people worldwide accessed Bitcoin in 2019. Since most people don't understand it well enough to consider using it, it remains a mystery throughout the world. Around the world, less than 5 percent of the population owns any form of cryptocurrency. This includes the vast majority of small and medium-sized businesses, which are also slow to adopt and benefit from the blockchain technology and cryptos as legal tender.

9. Blockchain technology is still developing.

The blockchain networks are in their infancy of development with programmers and developers continually adding features and applications. This means that programming errors and system design faults are a part of the growing pains for establishing a solid network.

10. Massive energy consumption by miners.

Decentralized blockchain networks eat up enormous amounts of energy in order for transactions to be recorded, verified and stored. Miners who maintain the blockchain network won't continue to do so if they're not fairly compensated for their energy expenditures. This is in part why cryptocurrency users must pay transaction fees when using any blockchain network.

Many of the risks outlined above stem from the fact that the crypto industry is in its infancy and is still experiencing many different types of growing pains. This alone may be enough to dissuade novice investors from getting involved in this new asset class. To help you decide as to whether or not cryptos are an investment class you would like to invest in now or in the future, here are some sound reasons as to the potential rewards:

Rewards:

1. High Returns.

In the short term, wide fluctuations in a coin's price can offer up high returns for the adept trader or knowledgeable investor. And for a buy-and-hold investor, any popular, well-established cryptocurrency historically will yield good returns long term. Whether you plan on dabbling in trading or investing for the long haul, the key to success in any market is to conduct enough research about each coin to fully understand the upside and downside risks each one has to offer. As well, you should commit to tracking your holdings on a regular basis so as to mitigate any chances of serious loss. In times of economic instability, high potential returns are definitely an attractor factor.

2. Ease of transfer at reasonable rates.

Digital transfers between two parties are quick and relatively easy. Transaction fees are also very low compared to typical bank charges and transfers. Instead of having to dish out $20 to $30 for many international transactions, you'll be paying fractions of a penny on the dollar. This is in part because a third-party overseer would take their cut from any transactions processed through a bank. For example, credit card companies have to provide internal measures that guarantee you won't be charged twice, and that the vendor is operating in an ethical manner. Credit card fraud is on the rise and so too is the cost of doing business and the fees being charged to offset these measures. This is where cryptos have an advantage.

3. Security of Transactions.

Since both ends of each transaction are protected by the verification process inherent in the system, it becomes a "trust less" system. No need for either party to place their trust in each other or even have a high degree of trust between the parties. The human element of trust is taken out of the equation. A blockchain system ensures the security and integrity of all transactions, not a human being. Blockchain technology makes cryptos very secure from hacking or theft. Your funds are safer than in a bank, especially when you hold your coins offline in a "cold" storage wallet.

4. Transparency for all transactions.

Blockchain technology uses a public ledger, which is available to all its users to see. The data from each transaction or block is verified and time stamped before becoming a part of the chain. Since it cannot be tampered with, the network becomes trustworthy and highly secure. It doesn't need a third party to oversee the network. For example, since 2009, Bitcoin has not required any third party to arbitrate any kind of transaction or dispute. The cost of doing business just got easier through crypto networks.

5. Fast transactions anywhere in the world.

Transactions can occur as quickly as in a few seconds or within minutes internationally. Both the business and the consumer need not wait days for transactions to clear as is the case for traditional financial institutions offering bank transfers or even credit cards. The authorization and issuance of funds used for crypto transactions happens almost instantaneously.

6. Easy to get started investing.

All that's required is access to some software, somewhere to store your money and a little knowledge. No need for special regulations or certificates, nor do you need to report to anyone and ask permission. Think of how complex the current system is in place for opening either a bank account or credit card. Not only does it take a lot longer to set up your accounts, but the amount of personal information being shared, and credit checks done can be unnerving. Also, being a simpler process gives developing nations a huge advantage where many individuals are unable to qualify for a bank account. Cryptos make saving and investment a reality for many of these individuals who are unbanked.

7. The banksters can't touch you.

Cryptocurrency trading occurs entirely outside of any direct control of national banks. Banks cannot freeze or seize your crypto accounts. They cannot touch your coins and tokens. Once you purchase cryptos on an exchange you have two choices: hold them on the exchange in a cloud-based digital wallet or transfer the coins to a wallet only you have access to. This could be a cold storage wallet, which is a small hardware device that can hold your coins offline. Or it could be a hot storage wallet that you've set up on your computer, tablet or smart phone that allows you to connect to the Internet. In either case, your funds cannot be frozen or confiscated, unless a government hit squad comes knocking on your door.

8. Greater control over financial transactions.

When you use your credit card the retailer is going to "pull" money from your card. In essence they have access to the full amount of credit remaining that's available on your card. Cryptos "push" transactions instead. You control the exact amount being delivered to any recipient. They don't have access to any other additional personal information in the transaction. As well, businesses accepting crypto payments pay transaction fees that are significantly lower than the 3 to 5 percent fees charged by credit card companies for each transaction.

9. Good storage of value.

Having a controlled supply of coins can boost the value of certain cryptos over time. The vast majority of cryptos have a special piece of source code that specifies how much can exist. Because of a limited supply, the intrinsic value of the crypto is easier to maintain, as opposed to a fiat currency where the more notes and coins being printed and in circulation, the less value they hold. With trillions of new dollars flooding the US economy in 2020 and 2021, we're seeing the price of goods rise. Any investment vehicle that is highly correlated to the US dollar must offer higher potential returns in order to beat the rate of inflation and attract investors.

10. Low inflation risk.

Traditional fiat currencies suffer from inflation losing their purchasing power or value during inflationary periods. Some countries, like Argentina, which suffers from a high rate of inflation, have adopted crypto payments for simple transactions like paying for public transportation. Argentina is not alone. Many countries in South America have been severely impacted by the economic fallout of the global pandemic. Citizens are investing in cryptos to sidestep the hyperinflation their country is currently experiencing.

11. Cryptos are easy to carry.

A million dollars of Bitcoin can be conveniently stored on a memory stick and carried in your pocket. Try to do that with a million dollars of the US greenback. In general, large amounts of cryptos are easier to carry around than fiat currencies having an equivalent value. In a crypto friendly world, no longer will consumers need to carry a billfold of cards and cash or a pocket full of coins. Transactions can be done from the convenience of one's mobile device.

12. Excellent source for mobile payments.

Multinational companies can now offer payment solutions for cross border shopping that eliminate the need to pay high transaction or currency conversion fees. Digital currency platforms eliminate the need to carry cash or bank cards. And mobile phone payments using a cryptocurrency are more secure than traditional online banking transactions.

13. Easily divisible into fractional units.

A cryptocurrency's value is calculated precisely to the last decimal point available. The value isn't rounded up or down as is the case for the US dollar, which can only be broken down to $1/100^{th}$ of a dollar. Many coins can be broken down to $1/1,000,000^{th}$ of a coin. This makes partial ownership of very, very, small quantities of a particular coin possible. It's also an important consideration should the value of any particular crypto skyrocket in price. The accurate value of the coin being held is precisely reflected in the pricing.

As more and more people worldwide interact with each other online, digital currencies become a more attractive option given all of the benefits previously mentioned. For this reason, the exponential growth of cryptos is here to stay. Now, that you have an understanding as to the major risks and rewards that cryptocurrencies offer, it's time to set up your investment portfolio the right way.

∽

BUILDING YOUR INVESTMENT PORTFOLIO

Before you allocate any funds to any particular investment opportunity, there is one critical factor that comes into play as to how successful that investment will become down the road. It all boils down to your understanding of the ins and outs as to how that investment vehicle works, along with those specific strategies that'll deliver the results you desire. This can only be accomplished by improving your financial education.

Education first:

Your first order of business before investing in any one particular asset class should be in improving your financial education. When you picked up this cryptocurrency investment guide, you did just that. You're in the process of empowering yourself to become a better investor. I encourage you to systematically invest in your financial education. Watch YouTube documentaries, read various investment books, listen to audiobooks and check out websites offering insights into the investing world. By the end of this book, you'll be in a better position to make sound decisions pertaining to the cryptocurrency market. But it's only the beginning of your journey.

As you increase your financial IQ, you'll be in a better position for solving any money problems you may be saddled with right now. And by improving the quality of the information you digest over time, you'll be capable of discerning between fact and opinion, which can have a dramatic effect on your financial affairs. You'll be tapping into your financial genius when making financial decisions that'll impact your life.

Whether or not you decide to put your hard-earned dollars into one investment class, or another, will ultimately be up to you. You may decide that after exploring your options for each investment vehicle, you feel more comfortable with one class over another. What's important to realize is that you're doing your due diligence for each possibility before jumping in.

As you explore the wonderful world of investing, you'll quickly discover that some investment vehicles require a different skill set, time commitment and capital exposure than other asset classes. These factors may deter you initially from getting involved. That's understandable.

As you move forward on your investment journey, your level of understanding will also change over time. Be patient with the overall learning process. Take your time getting your feet wet when you do start out. It's the combination of experience coupled with knowledge that'll give you the wisdom to generate consistent, sustainable returns down the road.

Diversification across Asset Classes.

In order to best achieve sustainable wealth over time, your cryptocurrency investments should be a part of a greater investment plan. Smart experienced investors don't put all of their eggs in one basket. They tend to choose several asset classes to invest in, such as a combination of bonds, stocks, commodities and real estate. In fact, rarely do you see any successful long-term investor allocating more than 50 percent to any one asset class.

Most investors are looking for investment vehicles that eventually will generate a steady income stream to support their desired lifestyle. This means that they're looking at acquiring certain assets that'll help them with the process. Experienced investors focus on those classes that have a proven track record of generating cash flow from the investment. And, what you're about to discover in this guide is just how to do that with your crypto positions.

Let's take a quick look at the four most popular asset classes that the general population typically invest their money in. This'll set the stage as to how you could structure your overall investment portfolio over time.

1. Bonds.

A bond is a fixed-income investment whereby you're promised a certain rate of return for holding this investment instrument until maturity. Bonds are thought to be a lower risk investment compared to most other investment classes. Unfortunately, in today's economic climate long-term government bonds have low yields, being just above the rate of inflation. Over the past thirty years bonds have historically produced an average rate of return of 5 to 6 percent. Generally, the less stable the issuer, the higher the yield that'll be paid out to the bondholder. With greater default risk, a higher rate of return is necessary in order to entice investors. Also, the longer the bond's term, the more attractive the yield. Since your money is being tied up for a longer period of time, investors want to be compensated for the lack of liquidity.

2. Stocks.

Most people are familiar with the stock investing world. They may have holdings through their employer's benefit package such as a 401K. Historically, a well-diversified portfolio of individual stocks has generated an average annual return between 9 and 10 percent over the past thirty years. If you're a patient passive buy and hold investor this strategy can generate a significant rate of return. Should you be an actively engaged stock investor who also uses conservative options strategies with positions they control, you can realize returns that double those traditionally experienced by passive investors. What separates the two investors in my mind is knowledge. Generating a monthly stream of income from the options market not only accelerates your wealth creation potential but by selling option contracts you actually build in downside protection for your holdings. Should you like some additional insights into this aspect of the stock market, check out the book or audiobook "Cash Flow Stock Investing".

3. Commodities.

From pork bellies to precious metals there's a host of commodity markets to play in. Most investors are familiar with gold and silver investments. They have served as a hedge against inflation and the constant erosion of the value of major fiat currencies. In the short-term precious metal markets can be volatile, yet long-term they've maintained their value and are therefore a possible investment worth considering. They hold their value over time because of the limited supply in circulation. Precious metals have become more difficult to find and extract. Their scarcity and high demand keep the price propped up. Most commodity markets have seen average annual rates of return over the past 40 years of slightly above 10 percent.

When we compare cryptocurrencies, which have been likened to owning digital gold, to precious metals, we see some of the same market characteristics. Both are scarce or in limited supply. Both are a hedge against inflation and the devaluation of the dollar. And both are a long-term storage of value. Where cryptos have the upper hand is that in being digital they are easier to store, transport and physically move from one end of the globe to the other. Being such a new commodity, they also have the distinct benefit of having produced annual returns of over 100 percent since 2010.

4. Real Estate.

Owning cash flowing rental property has been a popular investment vehicle amongst those with deeper purse strings who want to invest directly in the market. Real estate investment has blossomed over the past decade in part due to this asset class's ability to generate positive cash flow, the tax benefits afforded, the appreciation potential of the property's value and its stability as an investment class. On the flip side real estate typically has a high entry cost, requires active management and you run the risk of having to deal with bad tenants. Rental property is not a liquid asset and it does come with unexpected extra costs.

These four general asset classifications have traditionally found themselves into investment portfolios. Which asset classes you choose to explore and eventually hold is primarily up to what you're the most comfortable with. You'll need to take into consideration some of the following key factors before jumping in:

- How much time you're willing to spend initially finding, assessing and acquiring the underlying asset.
- How much time you can actually spend monitoring and managing

the asset.
- How long you intend on holding the asset.
- How much downside risk you're willing to assume.
- How much initial seed capital you require to get started.
- What reasonable rate of return you're expecting to generate.

You should take a serious look at these six factors on your own by doing some in-depth research before putting any skin in the game. Which brings us to your own investment philosophy.

Establish Your Own Investment Philosophy:

As Robert Kiyosaki points out in his book "Rich Dad's Guide to Investing":

"It's not the investment that's risky. It's the investor."

What he's referring to is that investment risk can be mitigated by improving the quality of one's financial education. As your understanding of how a market works, the better you become at entering and exiting the market in a profitable position. This is why spending the time now learning about various investment vehicles will help you formulate a successful overall investment philosophy. As I've always said:

"Learn before you earn."

As you gain knowledge and couple that with experience in the market, you'll discover that your comfort level with risk also increases. Now, I'm not saying that you'll become a reckless, risk averse investor. On the contrary, you'll assess investment opportunities in a different light. Those opportunities that appear to be riskier on paper will require more of your attention in doing your due diligence to reduce exposure and the potential for loss.

How you go about allocating funds for cryptocurrency investments should be based on three key criteria:

1. Liquidity preference.
2. Time preference.
3. Risk preference.

1. Liquidity Preference.

Most investors like to have a high degree of control over their investments. They want to be able to quickly get in and get out of trades, no matter what the market is doing. Those cryptocurrencies that offer this degree of liquidity are the market leaders like Bitcoin and Ether. Any of the top 10 coins by market cap should offer this level of flexibility. Incidentally market cap or capitalization is the total value attributed to a particular coin or token. It's calculated by multiplying the current price of the coin by the number of coins in active circulation. Market cap is an indicator of the market size for a particular coin.

2. Time Preference.

Every market goes through a market cycle with an upward trend known as the bull or expansion phase and a downtrend or bear market phase. Knowing which part of the cycle you'll be investing in; will influence how you allocate your funds. Also, how long you're willing to commit to a particular coin or token before cashing out also factors into your time decision. As a general rule, the longer your holding period or time horizon, the less of a factor market timing becomes in your overall strategy.

3. Risk Preference.

Risk is very personal and subjective. What one might consider to be a risky position, may be acceptable for a seasoned knowledgeable investor. Risk also is a factor that takes on new meaning when looking at it from the perspective of the market cycle. For example, one's position might be deemed to be a riskier one at the tail end of a two-year bull runup in the markets. Investing after a major market correction takes on a different risk tolerance profile.

Using these three criteria in tandem should provide you with a better indication as to how you'll allocate your funds over time and through various market cycles.

As a novice or intermediate level cryptocurrency investor there are three philosophical approaches to investing in cryptos which you should be familiar with. Each has its place in your arsenal of potential investment approaches you can tap into once you're more comfortable with what each has to offer. These three approaches are:

1. Hodling Coins and Tokens.
2. Swing Trading Positions.
3. Speculative Growth Plays.

1. Hodling Coins and Tokens.

Similar to the buy and hold approach to investing in the stock market, hodling is the long-term crypto investment strategy that has you holding onto a position until the asset becomes impaired.

This is the investment strategy touted by MicroStrategy CEO Michael Saylor. His simple four-step philosophical investment approach is to:

*   Find scarce, desirable, unimpaired assets.
*   Hold the asset for 100 years.
*   Borrow against these assets when you need capital.
*   Sell the asset when it becomes impaired.

He has heavily invested in Bitcoin over the past year. Bitcoin is a scarce, limited supply, globally popular, decentralized monetary instrument that has generated positive returns long-term. He intends on holding on his Bitcoin positions until the asset class no longer is capable of generating consistent positive returns long-term. He has already mentioned that should he require capital from his holdings, he will simply use his Bitcoin as collateral and borrow against the asset to obtain any fiat currency he may need in the future.

This philosophical approach should be a significant part of your overall investment strategy as you make your first few crypto investments. Most crypto investors with a solid track record through at least one crypto market cycle would also concur with Michael Saylor's buy and hold approach.

Initially, 100 percent of your coin acquisitions may end up being allocated as hodling positions. Over time, as your understanding of how crypto markets function, you may decide to reduce this percentage.

2. Swing Trading Positions.

Swing trading involves moving into and out of the market when certain target price points have been met trading a particular coin or token. The core premise is that you buy the dips in the market and sell the highs. With the crypto marketplace being so volatile, this can be an effective strategy to employ when you understand investor sentiment and the emotional roller coaster ride of the markets.

Swing trading requires an in-depth understanding of technical indicators and charts that'll help predict entry and exit points for occasionally trading coin or token positions. Unlike day trading whereby you may be preoccupied with entering and exiting positions several times during the course of a day, swing trading tries to capture longer market moves as the market swings from being overbought to oversold.

This approach to investing in cryptos can be more lucrative in the short-term. It's a popular approach used by more seasoned investors who are riding up a bull market, then pulling the plug along the way up by selling their positions. They'll just wait for the market to self-correct and buy back in when the coin or token they're trading can be picked up at a discount to their sell price.

With swing trading the timeframe of buying and selling transactions could be a year or two apart if you're using a market cycle as your framework. But more realistically, a swing trader is looking to capture market gains over a period of weeks or months.

Should this investment approach intrigue you, start by learning technical analysis, followed by a longer market cycle trade. This'll give you the experience of moving into and out of the market based on your read of the market cycle. There's less chance of significant capital loss when you're playing with the timeframe of an entire four-year market cycle.

Once you've gained the knowledge and experience to move effectively into and out of your initial market cycle positions, consider shortening your timeframe. For example, when I invest in the stock market, I often select companies that also trade in the options market. I'll purchase shares of a company and sell monthly covered calls on my position. Selling calls in the options market is a conservative options trading approach, not unlike the swing trading approach I'm advocating for a knowledgeable intermediate crypto investor. You could theoretically swing trade using a monthly or bi-monthly schedule based on how the market is moving.

Assuming that you would like to dabble in swing trading down the road, it's best to scale into this investment style slowly over time. The markets are going nowhere. You'll have plenty of opportunities to explore swing trades over the course of a year. What's important is to ensure that you diversify your positions and also allocate a portion of your portfolio to a long-term hodling position. Many seasoned investors like to keep at least 50 percent of their portfolio set aside for hodling.

3. Speculative Growth Plays.

With the number of coins and tokens a crypto investor could conceivably invest in approaching 10,000, investment opportunities can present themselves with some in-depth research.

The notion of making speculative investments is not much different than investing in penny stocks in the stock market. Some of these investment opportunities have the potential to generate significant returns, evolving into incredibly lucrative growth plays. Unfortunately, most crash and burn fading away out of existence.

In this guide, you'll be presented with enough insights and tools to be able to start doing the due diligence necessary for assessing potential growth opportunities. As with investing in penny stocks, making small capital investments in coins or tokens that could 10x over a short period of time is enticing.

Should you decide to integrate investing in speculative growth plays into your particular investment approach, do so with small positions. As the word "speculative" should warn you, please don't invest capital that you cannot afford to lose. When I invest in anything speculative, I ensure that I've spent hours doing my own due diligence on the opportunity before committing any hard cold cash. I never place my faith in others doing a deep dive into the investment for me. Talk is cheap. Beware of shady promoters pumping and dumping any asset.

Since these plays are not capital intensive, one can allocate a smaller percentage of one's overall portfolio to speculation. A number often tossed around investment circles is to keep these types of plays under 10 percent of one's overall portfolio makeup.

An Overview of the Investment Approach:

Since this guide focuses on the cryptocurrency market, let's look at those steps you could and should take when investing for the long-haul. Your initial focus for your investment portfolio will be to set up your various accounts. Here's an overview of what you'll be doing that's covered in each of the following chapters:

Step 1: Set up secure platforms and accounts.

For reasons that will be made clear later, ideally, you'll set up cryptocurrency accounts on at least two popular global exchanges. But before you do that, we'll ensure that you've secured your computer. Once your computer has been set up, you'll also create a secure email account and integrate two-factor authentication into all of your devices, especially your mobile phone.

Step 2: Protect your crypto investments.

Your next consideration is determining whether or not you'll invest in a cold storage wallet to protect any of your coins or tokens offline. You may not see the value of using a hardware wallet when you first start investing in cryptos; however, as you're about to discover they're handy when you want to exit the market and cash in your coins and tokens when the markets are heated.

Step 3: Don't save money. Save cryptos instead.

This is more of a mental shift than anything else. With the buying power of fiat currency diminishing, moving a portion of your cash savings from your financial institution to an exchange and investing in cryptos could potentially grow your savings over time. Bank interest rates are dismal. Cryptos held long-term through market cycles offer greater upside potential.

Step 4: Focus on Market Leaders.

A major part of your overall crypto portfolio should be invested in a couple of tried-and-true market leaders having a strong reputation for sustainable growth. Two we'll explore below are Bitcoin and Ethereum's Ether.

Step 5: Diversify Your Holdings.

Not only should you diversify your crypto holdings across several popular coins or tokens, but you should consider diversifying your exposure to cryptos in other ways. This can be accomplished by setting up an investment account with an online discount broker.

Besides opening a cryptocurrency account on at least one exchange, you should consider setting up an investment account that can hold several different asset classes, like a Roth IRA. A Roth IRA allows you to build up tax-free wealth over time through stock and bond holdings. Money deposited into a Roth IRA is pre-taxed. This means that any capital growth over time is tax exempt. And that's an attractive feature to have down the road when you'll need to withdraw a portion of your holdings over time.

As of this writing, an IRA account allows anyone who has earned income to invest up to $6000 per year. That is unless you're 50 years or older, in which you can invest up to $7000 per annum. You can contribute up to the full amount as long as your taxable income as an individual filer doesn't exceed $125,000 or $198,000 for married couples filing jointly.

Setting up a Roth IRA can give you much greater flexibility as to the types of investments you can hold in your account. You may decide at some point in time that you would like to invest in individual stocks of Blockchain companies or a Bitcoin ETF to diversify your exposure to the cryptocurrency market. A Roth IRA allows you to do so with the added advantage of any gains being generated being tax exempt.

Step 6: Consider setting up a decentralized finance (DeFi) account.

At some point in time, your crypto portfolio will have appreciated in value to a point whereby you would like to access some of the capital gains you've accumulated. Rather than withdraw huge portions of your crypto portfolio and have to pay capital gains taxes, as well as give up control over the underlying asset, there is another option. You can lend out your crypto on a lending platform thus generating a regular stream of income in the process. Or you could use your crypto as collateral for a loan and use the cash proceeds to fund a major investment or purchase.

As you can see, learning how to set up various accounts and platforms will empower you to better manage your cryptocurrency holdings now and well into the future. Let's explore two market leaders all diversified investors should hold in their crypto portfolios.

Investing in the Market Leaders Bitcoin and Ether:

Once you have taken the time to set up secure platforms, your exchange and investment accounts, it's now the moment you've been waiting for. Which coins should I consider investing in? Let's take a look at the top two coins in the crypto marketplace.

1. Bitcoin.

By far the most dominant coin in the digital currency landscape is Bitcoin. It has been one of the best long-term investments in the crypto market since its inception in 2009. It was the first coin to be implemented as a medium of exchange and storage of long-term value. As American billionaire entrepreneur Mark Cuban pointed out in an April 1, 2021 interview:

> "Bitcoin is a crypto asset. It's not a currency and it's not going to be a currency. It is a store of value."

For this reason, Bitcoin has grown to be the dominant cryptocurrency asset over the past decade. And every investor should hold a position in this cryptocurrency. It's like investing in a market leader such as Google, Amazon, Facebook, or Apple.

What's also important to understand about the crypto market is that in the early years the market movers were the retail (do-it-yourself) investors as opposed to large institutional buyers like hedge funds, pension plans and corporations. Much of the volatility in the markets could be attributed to retail investors trading the dips and upswings. Very few buy-and-hold institutional investors had taken any positions in the market.

By mid 2020, we saw an increased interest by institutional buyers to stockpile cryptocurrencies as many believed that the market would offer more attractive returns long-term than traditional bond and equity markets. This coin will continue to garner investor attention even more so from large institutional players looking to capitalize on what it has to offer. Compared to holding corporate cash in fiat currency backed instruments like bonds, Bitcoin offers institutional investors a lot more advantages for not only preserving capital but also growing and protecting it from the erosive effects of inflation. This means that Bitcoin is the Gold Standard of cryptocurrencies.

2. Ether.

As we've seen, Ethereum is a programmable blockchain that developers can use to build programs for specific applications in the business world and society. It has been gaining a lot of programmer and developer support in recent years because of its ability to use smart contracts for many traditional decision-making operations.

Of note is that the Enterprise Ethereum Alliance (EEA) is going to be a key driver in the adoption of Ethereum globally. It's made up of an advisory group of big businesses like Microsoft, J.P. Morgan and FedEx.

In a YouTube interview on March 29, 2021 on the U-Related channel about the digital renaissance age, retired hedge fund manager Raoul Pal said:

> "Everything is going to change. It's not just how we bank, how we transfer money, how we store value. We're moving into a truly digital world of which everything around us will change."

He goes on to say:

> "Ethereum is going to play a large role."

Currently, hundreds of coins and tokens are built on the Ethereum platform. This means that they all potentially share one common coin for transactions, that being Ether. Ethereum is currently undergoing a series of updates over the next couple of years in order to improve the network's ability to scale and work more efficiently.

The next Ethereum upgrade, called EIP-1559, is scheduled to go live in Ethereum's "London" hard fork in July 2021. This hard fork or major infrastructure change will lower the volatility of transaction fees and move Ethereum in the direction of becoming a deflationary asset. For these reasons, a smart investor should allocate a significant portion of their portfolio in Ether behind Bitcoin.

Coin and Token Allocation:

When you first get started investing in cryptocurrencies, your focus will initially be on building a position in Bitcoin and Ether, the two top popular and highly successful coins with proven track records. These two cryptos may be the only one's you're holding onto in the beginning.

As you systematically move your fiat currency from low interest-bearing bank accounts onto exchanges where the cash can be quickly allocated for crypto purchases, you'll want to expand your selection of holdings so you can take advantage of future growth prospects from upcoming coins and tokens. For the more prudent and conservative investor this may mean just sticking to those coins that appear in the top 10 by market cap. This information can be found on a site like Coin Market Cap (https://www.coinmarketcap.com).

A conservative investor might allocate 50 percent or more of his or her portfolio to Bitcoin and Ether. The balance of the portfolio could be split up amongst another two or three top 10 picks. This approach simplifies the selection and allocation process and is well suited for the hodler or novice investor. When you prefer not taking an active role in your crypto investing, then this more laid-back approach is appropriate. This approach can be likened to that of the passive investor in the stock market who invests in value stocks.

As your knowledge and interest in cryptocurrency investing blossoms, you may eventually feel that you would like to take a more active role in your investing by either:

- Trading a portion of your portfolio holdings with the occasional swing trade.
- Or finding upcoming coins and tokens with huge upside growth potential.

For this reason, this guide covers some of the basic selection criteria you'll need to integrate into your assessment of potential crypto plays. Start by whetting your appetite into what it'll take as far as tools and criteria you'll need to reference in order to make sound decisions. I would encourage you to also spend some time exploring other educational resources that'll give you a broader perspective and understanding of what to focus your attention on.

Key to your ongoing success will be to what degree you're willing to improve your financial IQ. With that notion in mind, as you venture out exploring what either swing trading or speculative investment plays have to offer, start slowly. Begin by allocating only a small percentage of your overall portfolio to these pursuits. You will make investment mistakes. We all do. Learn from them before allocating a larger portion of your portfolio to "active investing".

It's important to allocate the majority of your overall crypto portfolio to market leaders. Keep any speculative investments to a minimum, until you've become familiar and successful with the whole process of selecting, entering and exiting profitable positions.

Now that you have a better notion as to how you should build your overall crypto investment system, let's take a deep dive into each aspect from setting up secure accounts to determining how and when you should exit your positions.

~

SETTING UP SECURE ACCOUNTS

Investing in cryptocurrencies comes with risks, which need to be mitigated as much as possible. The biggest threat is ensuring that your cryptos are being held in a secure location out of the reach of hackers. It's up to you to take all of the necessary steps to protect your investments. You'll discover that when things go really wrong there is no government agency you can go to for help, nor are there any legal recourses you can pursue in the case of loss. This is why you'll need to take several precautionary steps in advance before you invest in any cryptocurrency. Here are six specific steps to take BEFORE buying cryptos:

Step 1: Use paper notebooks for storing sensitive information.

The safest way to keep all of your crypto related information private and secure is by recording all of your important passwords, login details, account particulars, and transactions in a notebook. This ensures that the most important information about your accounts and holdings is stored off the Internet and you have 100 percent control of it.

Since you'll be recording information crucial to accessing your crypto investments, you should take the extra precaution of creating a backup copy or ledger of your notebook.

Your notebook will be used to store:

- all account login credentials,
- passwords,
- transaction information
- crypto wallet and exchange information.

You should avoid storing any passwords, account logins or transaction details online, on your phone or on any device directly connected to the Internet.

Store both your journals in separate locations as you never know when an unforeseen disaster may affect either your home or office. Having a fire-proof safe at home adds another layer of protection against disasters.

Also consider entering your contact details and an offer of a financial reward should your journal be lost in transit anywhere.

As well, should something happen to you down the road and you become incapacitated, try to provide a few detailed notes or instructions in your journal as to how to safely access, transfer and cash in your funds. This'll make it much easier for family and friends to figure out your financial affairs. You may wish to consider typing up these instructions and slipping a printed copy into each of your journals before deleting your file.

Step 2: Create secure passwords for your cryptocurrency accounts.

Long, complicated passwords with no recognizable pattern are the best way of securing your crypto accounts and wallets. Hackers use sophisticated programs that run through common passwords and combinations of characters. You need to make your passwords as long and random as possible using a combination of upper- and lower-case letters, numbers and symbols.

You'll also want to avoid using an online service that generates random strings of characters for you. You don't know if the site is secretly storing these "random" passwords or not.

As well, don't use the same password for more than one account. You want to maintain a high degree of security for each and every one of your password-protected applications. And avoid storing your passwords on your browser. Can you see how a notebook will prove useful in storing all of this data?

Avoid using:

- common phrases.
- anything resembling a word or sentence.
- reverse order words.

If any of your accounts require a security question, use the same approach for creating each answer as you'll be doing for your passwords. Create long complex answers that contain fake information.

Step 3: Secure your computer before buying cryptocurrency.

The first order of business is to consider investing in a UPS backup battery to protect your computer hardware should you experience a power surge or blackout. The UPS unit will provide you with enough of a power supply to save any crypto data or transactions you may be working on.

The second order of business is setting up a strong password to access your computer. Do this now and record your password and creation date in your notebook.

Before setting up any crypto accounts or wallets for holding your crypto purchases, you'll need to clean your computer of any malware. There are many free tools and services available for scanning, cleaning and securing. One popular platform to consider using is Malwarebytes. It allows you to use the premium program for 14 days for free, at which point it'll be ~$58 per year per device.

Step 4: Secure your smartphone before buying cryptocurrency.

If you plan to use your smartphone for accessing your cryptos, then you'll need to set up some additional security measures with your phone.

The first measure is to contact your cellphone provider and set up a passphrase that must be disclosed before activating a new SIM card on your account. Record this passphrase in your journal. This ensures that hackers trying to steal your phone's identity by requesting a new SIM card will be met with a roadblock.

The second measure to implement is to require a password to unlock your phone. Should your phone be lost or stolen, you've placed another layer of protection for accessing your investments.

It may also be prudent to remove your smartphone number from any social media platforms or public websites. You should never publish your cellphone number anywhere where people you don't trust may have access to it.

Companies like Malwarebytes also have security software for mobile devices you can install. This'll secure your smartphone even further.

Step 5: Create an encrypted email account.

To keep things better secured, now's the time to create a new email address that you haven't used before. Select a random handle to use with the account. One that hasn't been used before. Avoid using an existing email account that others know about. Privacy and security are paramount to keeping your investments safe.

If you're looking for a secure email provider that provides encrypted email accounts, then consider picking up a free basic account through ProtonMail out of Switzerland. Once you do set up your email account ensure that you jot down your username and password into your journal.

Step 6: Set up two-factor authentication applications.

Once you've secured your phone and computer, it's time to add two-factor authentication to them. Two-factor authentication (2FA) adds an additional layer of protection for accessing an account on any device connected to the Internet. The way it works is that once you've entered your password, you'll be prompted to input a code generated by your two-factor authentication app. It's usually a 6-digit random sequence of characters that changes every 20 to 30 seconds. This means that someone won't be able to access your account unless they physically have your cell phone at that particular moment.

You should consider setting up two different authentication apps that'll give you some flexibility moving forward as to which exchanges or platforms you'll be accessing in the future.

If you already have a Gmail account, Google Authenticator is a good choice. You'll need to go to the app store on your phone, type in Google Authenticator, and download the app. Once it downloads, you'll need to set it up on your devices using both your computer and smart phone.

You'll be given two set-up options: scan barcode and manual entry. From your computer go to your Internet browser, open your Google account security page using the URL: https://myaccount.google.com/security. Next, scroll down and open the 2-Step Verification section, which'll prompt you to enter your Google account password. Google will then send you either a text message or voice call to receive a verification code on your phone. Once you enter the code on your phone, you can now set up the particular type of phone you use, either Android or iPhone.

The next step is to synch your phone to the Authenticator app you've installed on your computer. It's a simple process. Just scan the barcode as if you're taking a picture of the code on the computer screen. Once successful, your phone will display the 6-digit code along with your Gmail address. Just enter this code on your computer and click 'verify".

As a final step, it's a good idea to go to the "Devices you trust" section in your Gmail account and choose "revoke all". In this way, no matter which device you decide to use for logging into your Gmail, two-step verification will be required.

Another two-factor authentication app to consider downloading is Authy, as not all crypto exchanges accept Gmail Authenticator. When you do install a second app onto your devices, keep in mind that you won't be able to use both apps with the same exchange account. It's an either or scenario.

The process for setting up Authy is very similar to Google's procedure. Here's how to set up Authy. First, go to the app store on your phone, type in Authy and download the app. Once downloaded, enter your smart phone number, email address you created in ProtonMail or Gmail, get the account verification via a phone call or text message, and enter your registration code being sent.

In Authy, enable App Protection in the Security section of the Authy app and enter a 4-digit pin of your choice. Record the login details and pin number in your journal. Also, enable "protect entire app" in the security section of the Authy app. This process secures the Authy app.

Next, exit the "Security" section and click on the "Accounts" icon to set up an "Authenticator backup". Choose a long, strong backup password and once enabled, write this down in your journal.

The following step is optional. Should you like to increase your app's security, then open the "Devices" icon and disable "allow multi-device" option. If you leave this option enabled, you'll be able to log into your Authy app from any device.

You now have two authenticator apps enabled on your smart phone. Time to set up two-factor authentication for your ProtonMail account, if you've set this account up.

Once you log into your email account, go to "Settings", choose the "Security" tab, and click "Enable Two-Factor Authentication". Open your 2FA app on your cell phone using Authy, scroll down and choose "Add Account", then scan the QR code. Authy will prompt you to name the account.

Back on ProtonMail, enter your current password followed by the two-factor authentication passcode displayed on your smart phone in Authy. Remember this code changes every 20 to 30 seconds, so you don't want to dilly dally. Once you click "Submit", ProtonMail will provide you with several one-time use recovery codes. Copy these down in the order they're listed into your paper journal. Should you lose your phone and be unable to access your authenticator app, these recovery codes provide you access.

I realize that I've taken some time explaining in detail various levels of security you should set up in advance before purchasing any cryptos. Preventing others from accessing your cryptocurrency holdings may not be a big deal when you get started investing; however, over time your holdings might grow to a sizeable amount. Securing your holdings will become paramount then.

⌇

CRYPTOCURRENCY EXCHANGES

You have two general options as to how to go about buying and selling cryptocurrencies. By far the most popular approach is to go through an exchange that specializes in trading cryptos. These trading platforms connect buyers to sellers and usually levy a transaction fee to each user for each trade. The second approach is to do direct trading for individual-to-individual transactions across the globe. The peer-to-peer marketplace doesn't have a fixed market price. Buyers and sellers negotiate the exchange rate.

Much of the focus of this guide is on the use of established platforms within the cryptocurrency space. With this in mind, let's take a look at how to select an appropriate exchange for your particular interests and needs. When looking for an exchange for buying and selling cryptocurrencies, it's best to focus on answering the question: What's the best crypto exchange for me?

Needs and preferences vary from individual to individual. A buy and hold crypto investor touting the benefits of one exchange over another, may not have the same opinion about another exchange that meets the needs of someone dabbling in the occasional swing trade. For this reason, it would be more beneficial for you to get a feel for what some of the popular exchanges offer and then decide for yourself which platform checks off the most boxes. But before we do that there are some underlying questions, you'll want to keep top of mind before signing up for any exchange.

Selection Criteria for Choosing an Exchange:

Since it has been the Wild West over the past decade in the crypto space as far as reputable exchanges go, this has posed a challenge for many investors in being able to find an exchange that'll meet their needs.

Use this checklist to help you narrow down your choices as to what to look for before joining an exchange:

1. Reputation.

Exchanges that have a long track record tend to also be the most popular and reliable. Those that have a strong user participation rate and trading volume often are solid candidates. Check out Bitcoin forums on Reddit or Bitcointalk to get a feel for how the exchange might be doing in the market. Lots of negative feedback or complaints can signal more serious issues with the exchange.

2. Fees.

Ensure that all fees are transparent. It's important to understand the transaction fee and withdrawal fee process before investing. Fees can vary widely from one exchange platform to another. For example, the Canadian exchange BitBuy can cost you 4 percent in total fees should you deposit, buy, sell and withdraw funds for a position. Although this exchange is a popular, easy-to-use platform it does come with a cost. Fees can erode your portfolio over time, especially if you make more frequent transactions, which is a factor to consider should you be pursuing a more active role in your investing.

3. Payment Methods.

Find out what different payment methods are available to you when it comes to funding your crypto account with fiat currency. Limited options means increased inconvenience. You'll also want to verify if there are substantial fees being assessed for making either deposits or withdrawals. Verify and compare exchange rates being charged by each platform for fiat to digital currency transactions and vice-versa.

4. Verification Process.

Platforms that have a specific verification process want to protect you and the exchange from any scams or money laundering. Most centralized exchanges will require you to provide identification verifying your ID before making any deposits and withdrawals. Some exchanges require just a rudimentary level of personal information for opening an account. Others may require a more elaborate verification process often seen with financial institutions using KYC (know your client) guidelines.

As a rule of thumb to help with your decision-making, the more involved and complex the account verification and set-up process the more likely the exchange can offer a higher level of security for its members.

5. Geography.

Some exchanges are accessible only from certain countries. And some will offer various levels of service depending on your geographical location. You want your exchange to offer a variety of services for your country of residence.

6. Liability.

Unfortunately, much of the burden of responsibility in using a particular crypto exchange rests on the user's shoulders. Some exchanges do provide financial protection by insuring the more popular coins up to a point. This is currently the exception to the rule rather than general practice. It should be pointed out that cryptos operate outside of the control of a central government or financial institution. Therefore, the same level of financial protection offered by banks or stockbrokers may not exist in the world of cryptocurrencies.

This is why a strong case can be made for cryptocurrency investors to store their coin purchases in a wallet they control 100 percent access to rather than using the digital wallets offered on most exchanges.

7. Tools and Resources.

Determine what helpful tools and resources the exchange provides for its users. Technical analysis tools can vary widely from one exchange to the next. Fortunately, most novice investors will do just fine with the vast majority of the technical analysis charting tools available.

Top 5 Exchanges to Consider:

Based on the seven selection criteria that we've just outlined, here are five major exchanges to explore:

1. Coinbase Pro.

This San Francisco based exchange was one of the first to enter the crypto marketplace back in 2013. They are one of the largest exchanges with over 35 million users and over $220 billion in annual trade volume in 2020. According to Crunchbase data, the company is valued at $8 billion. They operate worldwide in over 100 countries.

You'll need to create a regular Coinbase account first before logging into Coinbase Pro. The Coinbase Pro trading platform allows you to place an assortment of trading orders such as market price, limit price and stop limit orders.

Depositing funds into Coinbase varies from country to country. For US-based investors you can use bank transfers, PayPal and Debit cards.

Fees can be divided into two main categories:

- Deposit and withdrawal fees.
- Trading fees.

For deposits and withdrawals, ACH (automated clearing house) is completely free. Swift deposits in Great Britain are also completely free; however, Swift withdrawals are charged 1 Quid. If you're looking to make a wire transfer, Coinbase charges a $10 deposit fee and $25 withdrawal fee. For most novice investors who'll be making a single deposit, this is probably the most cost-effective approach for one's initial deposit. And in Europe, SEPA transactions come with 0.15 Euro deposit and withdrawal fee.

What is good is that any cryptos taken off the exchange and stored on a cold storage device can be done so free of charge.

As for trading fees, if you're like most traders who are trading less than $10,000 per month there is a 0.5 percent trading fee for each transaction. This fee structure scales down with a higher trading volume. For example, someone trading $10,000 to $50,000 per month would incur trading fees of 0.35 percent.

An important consideration for many is the range of cryptocurrencies that can be traded on the platform. Fortunately, about 40 different cryptos are available for trading as of 2020.

Coinbase Pro has a support network up and running. Should you run into a problem or have a query, you can submit a support ticket form similar to sending an email message. Unfortunately, the support turn-around time is dismally slow. You can also get phone support Monday through Friday from 6 am to 6 pm Pacific Time.

As for security, 98 percent of user funds are held offline, which adds in another layer of security against theft or loss. Bitcoin is distributed geographically across the globe in safe deposit boxes and vaults. Both USB drives and paper backups are held. If you decide to keep your funds on an exchange, Coinbase is a secure option. Another feature worth mentioning is that Coinbase Pro has FDIC insurance of up to $250,000 for US customers. This is the same insurance used to protect bank customers.

One of the downsides of the Coinbase Pro platform has to do with the somewhat frequent temporary outages that occur with high market volatility that can be annoying to wait through, especially if there's a massive market move you want to capitalize on.

If you're looking to trade on the go, Coinbase Pro does have both IOS and Android apps you can install on any mobile device.

Being one of the easiest exchanges to use in the market it does come with a price - ease of use means higher fees. This platform is a great option for novice investors and not necessarily the best one for more experienced investors and traders.

2. Kraken.

Founded in 2011 by Jesse Powell, who used to trade at the Mt Gox exchange, this exchange is also based in San Francisco. Used by over 4 million active traders the company has a valuation of $4 billion making it one of the top three exchanges in North America.

Kraken keeps 95 percent of all deposits offline in an air-gapped distributed cold storage environment making it virtually impossible to hack and steal funds. The exchange's servers are also housed in secure, guarded cages that are under 24/7 surveillance by armed guards and video cameras. Physical access is highly controlled as is access to any data. All sensitive account information is encrypted at both the system and data levels.

Kraken doesn't have FDIC insurance like Coinbase Pro does. This is a consideration if you're a US citizen. However, they are one of the oldest, largest and most trusted crypto exchanges in the world. They encourage investors to not use their exchange as a savings institution but rather as a trading platform.

Since most people starting out with crypto investing prefer doing everything from one account if possible, having access to a multitude of cryptocurrencies is important. Kraken supports three dozen cryptos making it desirable for novice and intermediate level investors.

Kraken makes it easy for holders of foreign currencies to purchase coins, as the exchange supports US dollars, Euros, Canadian dollars, British pounds, Japanese yen and Swiss francs.

Kraken takes a restricted country approach as to who they'll accept as clients. However, they do offer exchange services in over 100 countries worldwide. US customers can make bank account deposits, whereas Canadian customers can also make cash and debit deposits. These are charged a modest $1.25 CDN + 0.25 percent in account deposit fees. For US-based customers, Kraken charges a flat fee of $5 USD for most wire transfers. Worldwide SWIFT deposits are also charged a flat fee of usually $5 USD per deposit.

Kraken uses a maker-taker fee schedule, as do many exchanges, with volume incentives based on your exchange activity level in the past 30 days. Maker fees are paid for orders that make liquidity. They are typically charged for limit orders that are away from the market rate. On the other hand, taker fees are paid when the investor removes any liquidity restrictions by placing a simple market order. In general, maker fees tend to be slightly lower than taker fees. For example, transactions under $50,000 will incur a maker fee of 0.16 percent while taker fees are slightly higher at 0.26%. This makes Coinbase Pro about twice as expensive as Kraken when comparing transaction fees.

When you purchase cryptos most novice investors place a "market" order. This type of order is executed quickly at the current market price for the coin or token. A "limit" order sets a price limit the investor is willing to buy or sell the coin or token at. In order for the transaction to occur the current price of the crypto must hit the limit price, then the limit order is processed as a market order in the marketplace.

As for liquidity in the crypto market, if a trade order is not matched immediately against an order already on the order book, this adds what is known as liquidity to the market. In other words, the opportunity to buy and sell that crypto has increased. Liquidity refers to the ease with which a crypto can be converted into cash as market price.

Registration on the Kraken platform is more involved than Coinbase Pro. You'll need to submit several documents for verification such as a valid government-issued identification document like a passport or driver's licence, a proof of residence document like a bank statement, utility bill or credit card statement, a valid Social Security Number and a face photo. You'll also need to disclose occupational information. This will allow you to deposit up to $100,000 USD into your account within any 24-hour period of time.

Kraken offers more options and flexibility when it comes to buying and selling cryptos on the exchange versus Coinbase Pro. You'll also have more tools available for trading and higher leverage amounts should you wish to trade on margin in the future.

Customer service on Kraken is solid, offering live chat support 24/7. This makes the platform one of the better exchanges in the marketplace when you need to resolve an issue or if you have specific questions.

The exchange does offer both desktop and mobile applications that allow you to trade from home or on the go with a smart phone. As with Coinbase Pro, Kraken provides more advanced day traders the option of setting up their own trading bots that allow for automatic programmable trading 24/7. And both exchanges do support third-party trading bot software.

Kraken offers both the novice and intermediate-level investor with a complete set of features, options and amenities, making it one of the top choices for any budding crypto investor to consider using.

3. Binance.

Several different versions of this exchange exist, such as Binance Singapore, Binance Uganda, and Binance US. These are different exchanges from Binance.com. Collectively, Binance is the largest exchange network in the world. It processes over $2 billion in transactions each day.

Binance.com has the most extensive crypto spot market in the world. It comes with a host of advanced trading tools. You also have the ability to trade on margin and get over-the-counter service to get better pricing for large volume transactions. Binance Earn provides you with the option of earning high interest rates with flexible savings accounts and DeFi staking. More on that in chapter 11, which looks at optimizing long-term returns.

The Binance Crypto Visa credit card gives you cashback of up to 8 percent. You also have access to flexible, collateralized crypto loans, which can be secured by your crypto holdings. You can even take part in exclusive ICO (Initial Coin Offerings) on the Binance Launchpad. As you can see there are a lot of unique features to Binance.

All crypto deposits are free and withdrawal fees are variable and dependent on the cryptocurrency or fiat currency you're getting off the exchange. They support some of the lowest fees for any major exchange. For example, base transaction fees are as low as 0.1 percent compared to the 0.5 percent fees charged by Coinbase Pro.

They offer a multitude of ways of making deposits from bank transfers to Visa and MasterCard charges.

As far as cryptocurrencies available on the exchange to trade, Binance is literally a buffet having hundreds at its disposal.

Customer support tends to be faster with turnaround times under 24 hours, unlike Coinbase's support ticket system.

Binance has apps for IOS, Android and desktop applications for Mac OS, Windows and Linux.

Binance does offer security support for cold storage hardware devices, multi-signature wallets, tiered access and enhanced cyber security detection systems. However, the exchange did get hacked in May 2019 for 7000 Bitcoins. Those users that were affected were reimbursed through Binance's SAFU fund. The good news is that 98 percent of all user funds are held offline in cold storage devices.

4. Uniswap.

This exchange launched in November 2018 even before decentralized finance became part of the mainstream cryptocurrency marketplace. Uniswap is a decentralized market-making exchange using an open-source DAPP (digital application protocol) built on the Ethereum network. A DEX, or decentralized exchange, allows you to exchange between two or more coins or tokens. Exchanges made on a DEX are done so in a peer-to-peer like fashion.

Uniswap allows you to swap Ether (ETH) for any ERC-20 token built on the Ethereum platform. This means that you're transferring the asset in a transparent way on the Ethereum blockchain. Unlike Coinbase Pro, which uses a centralized platform, Uniswap is decentralized. This means no company is holding onto your funds. You are always in control of your own assets. As well, Uniswap has an easy-to-use interface that also connects to popular Web 3.0 wallets like Metamask, Trust Wallet and Coinbase Wallet. These wallets are used to sign and authorize the DAPPs.

One tip for beefing up your crypto security on a DEX is to use a Web 3.0 wallet like Metamask in conjunction with a cold storage hardware device like a Ledger. This ensures that your private keys for your coins and tokens are offline until you need to move them.

You won't run into hacking and theft problems that plagued previous exchanges like Mt Gox, Quadrigacx and Cryptopia. All of these exchanges lost enormous amounts of investor capital due to thefts. This is why so many in the crypto space support decentralized exchanges like Uniswap. What's interesting to note is that Uniswap reported more trading volume than Coinbase in September 2020.

Liquidity pools is what makes Uniswap a decentralized platform. This means there are no country restrictions to speak of that'll regulate how the exchange functions and what information and protocols must be in place. Users can even earn trading fees by investing in pools of tokens which sit in smart contracts.

Unlike centralized platforms tied to government-controlled financial systems, Uniswap doesn't have the same degree of background checking done by other exchanges. There are no KYC (know your customer) information requirements seen with other more regulated and centralized exchange platforms. Government authorities cannot impose regulations and restrictions since DEXs have no central authority.

Being a non-custodial platform, there are no deposit or withdrawal fees. Instead, you'll pay Ethereum "gas" fees to send those tokens to the protocol and a 0.3 percent liquidity provider fee to swap tokens. This liquidity provider fee is immediately deposited into liquidity reserves. This increases the value of the liquidity tokens and functions as a payout to all liquidity providers who have invested in the pools of tokens.

Unfortunately, high Ethereum gas fees can cost you an arm and a leg if the network is super congested. Gas fees are paid to those miners who receive compensation for maintaining the Ethereum blockchain. Recall that gas refers to the unit that measures the amount of computational effort required to execute specific operations on the Ethereum network.

Being solely an ERC-20 crypto to crypto exchange, you'll need to already have some Ethereum or ERC-20 tokens already. No fiat deposits or withdrawals are available.

The big advantage is that hundreds of ERC-20 tokens are listed on the exchange for swapping. The downside is not being able to get your hands on any coins outside of the Ethereum ecosystem.

For mobile users, there isn't a dedicated mobile app you can access in order to initiate transactions from a smart phone or tablet. However, you can launch the app in your mobile browser and connect to a mobile wallet.

This exchange is a great complement to some of the other exchanges for an experienced investor looking to explore the token market, have control of their private keys and not entrust their funds to a centralized exchange.

5. FTX.

The final exchange to consider is one that most novice investors won't gravitate to. However, should you be considering trading cryptos in the future, FTX should be placed on your shortlist. This exchange was built with the advanced trader in mind. It was created in May 2019 in Antigua and Barbuda with offices based in Hong Kong. This trading platform has the support of Alameda Research, a quantitative trading firm that trades up to $1 billion per day and manages over $100 million in digital assets.

Unfortunately, FTX doesn't accept the residents of the United States, Cuba, Crimea, Iran, Syria, North Korea. and Antigua as of this writing. With the cryptocurrency space changing so rapidly this may change in the not-too-distant future as cryptos gain mainstream acceptance.

The platform has dozens of cryptos to choose from as well as future's markets to tap into along with an assortment of Indexes. For options traders, the platform provides access to Bitcoin options.

If you need to make large block trades, FTX has an over-the-counter platform set up that reduces transaction costs incurred. This makes it ideal for whales wanting to move large positions.

Fees are some of the lowest in the industry, understandably so since the exchange is being promoted to high volume traders. You can also benefit from getting further discounts by holding various amounts of the FTX token. For example, a $10,000 stake in the FTX token will grant you a 15 percent discount on any trading transaction fees.

Also deposits and withdrawals are free. FTX pays the withdrawal blockchain fees. If you're not going to trade much, FTX may assess a 0.10 percent withdrawal fee. This determination is based on your trade volume in comparison to the amount of fiat currency deposited.

Credit cards and wire transfers can be used for depositing and withdrawing a variety of fiat currencies. Withdrawals under $10,000 may incur a $75 fee, which is one limitation to be aware of.

FTX uses simple email support for resolving any issues.

As for security, FTX uses a cold storage protocol whereby most funds are stored offline, as is the case with most high-end exchanges today.

This platform is for experienced traders looking for exotic trading options like perpetual futures and leveraged tokens.

As I hinted at in Chapter 3, your exchange platform needs may change over time as both your portfolio and level of expertise grows. What may be fine right now may become inadequate later on. For most hodlers with small positions, an easy-to-use exchange platform will meet their immediate and future needs. However, if you plan on devoting more time and financial resources to cryptocurrency investing, then opening a couple of accounts may prove useful. This'll become more apparent when we explore exit strategies.

PROTECTING YOUR CRYPTOCURRENCIES

Hot versus Cold Storage Wallets:

There are two major types of cryptocurrency storage devices you should be aware of, namely hot and cold storage devices. These methods of storage are often referred to as wallets, which can lend to some confusion as a hot or cold storage wallet can contain several crypto wallets. It's like a dream within a dream from the Leonardo DiCaprio movie Inception.

To help differentiate between the two commonly used applications for the term wallet, I'll be referring to "crypto wallets" for holding specific coins and the term "hot or cold wallets" to refer to the method or type of storage device being used. In a nutshell, a "hot wallet" stores information online, whereas a "cold wallet" stores information offline. The safest way to store your cryptocurrencies is offline using hardware wallets, which function similar to a USB flash drive.

Hot wallets can be broken down into three categories. The first is a "desktop hot wallet", which is downloaded and installed on your computer device. You can access your cryptos using that particular device. These wallets are easy and convenient to use. However, should your computer be hacked, or you pick up a virus, you could end up losing all of your funds from the hack.

The second type of hot wallet is an "online software hot wallet" that is often a cloud-based storage device. Access to cloud-based storage can be done anywhere in the world from any device that can connect to the Internet. These types of wallets are similar to the addresses found on cryptocurrency exchanges. Often a third party is used to store your private keys online. When you own cryptos, you really own a private key that is a 256-bit number giving the owner access to those cryptos. As you can imagine, this is the least secure storage platform as they are extremely vulnerable to hackers.

The third type of hot wallet is a "mobile hot wallet", which is a mobile app stored on your smartphone. These wallets tend to be simple to use with limited features since they're operating on mobile devices with limited storage and display capabilities.

There are two general categories of "cold storage" devices or wallets being currently used. The first type of cold storage wallet is a "paper cold wallet", which holds the public and private keys accessing your crypto wallets. These wallets can come in the form of a QR code containing your public and private keys or a paper printout of your public and private keys or an engraved thin metal plate or card containing your keys. To access your funds, you'll need to either scan the QR code or manually type in the public and private keys.

They do offer a high degree of security since they reside offline. However, should your paper wallet be lost or destroyed by accident, you won't have access to your coins unless you have a backup in place, like your handwritten journal.

The second type of cold wallet device is a "hardware cold wallet" that stores information on a USB/flash drive-like device. When you're ready to send or receive funds, you plug in your hardware device into a computer or laptop that has access to the Internet. Storing your coins on this type of hardware storage device or wallet is the safest and most secure method of protecting your holdings.

Using Hardware Wallets for Storage:

When you're starting out in the crypto space, you may not be fully committed to the idea of investing in this relatively new asset class long term. In this case, finding a well-established exchange with a strong security reputation to both acquire cryptos and store them on their platform is a suitable option.

Start by selecting a regulated exchange that has known safety mechanisms in place.

Most digital exchanges do not go through the same scrutiny afforded other markets like the stock, options, bond or commodity exchanges. These particular markets undergo regular audits by well-known financial regulators.

Online storage with an exchange poses a risk of theft. This is why you should consider opting for online storage of your coins and tokens on a couple of different exchanges. This diversifies your risk of loss from hackers.

As your portfolio grows, you may reach a decision point as to whether or not you should invest in a cold storage hardware wallet to store all of your cryptocurrency. Although an inexpensive USB flash drive can be used, opt to purchase a dedicated cold storage device designed to store cryptocurrencies. They make the process much simpler and infinitely more secure.

Should you choose to use an ordinary USB storage device, back up your private keys to another platform. For example, if you go with a USB flash drive to store your transactions, consider having a backup in the cloud or with an exchange. If one wallet fails for whatever reason, at least you have access to the transactions on another platform.

Cold storage wallets use software to encrypt access to your device, which prevents third parties from accessing your device and robbing you blind.

They're also designed to protect your transactions should you plug your device into a compromised computer. These specialized devices do cost a few dollars but are worth the initial investment.

A cold storage device provides four key functions:

1. Stores your private and public keys used to access specific coins.
2. Smoothly interacts with the blockchain.
3. Monitors your account balances for each coin held.
4. Allows you to seamlessly send and receive cryptocurrencies.

How Do Wallets Work?

In order to access your bank account online, which holds your fiat currencies, there are two layers of protection normally installed - your bank account number and your online banking account application. Your banking app usually requires you to enter a username and password before granting you access to your bank account.

A cryptocurrency wallet functions in a similar way. The blockchain is represented by your banking institution. Your bank account number functions like your public key or what is often referred to as "addresses". Your bank app is your crypto wallet. And your online banking credentials can be likened to your private key for accessing your crypto wallet.

Your banking institution tracks and records all transactions going to and from your bank account. This is similar to the blockchain tracking and recording your crypto transactions going to and from your public key.

As well, your online banking app allows you to verify your account balances and send or receive transactions by entering your username and password. Your crypto wallet also allows you to check your balances and send or receive transactions once you enter your private key.

Contrast this with your public key. It acts like your bank account number, in which individuals can send you funds, but don't have access for withdrawing any funds. However, should you give someone access to your private key, they can access your account and send cryptocurrencies somewhere else. This is why it is so important to keep your private key private.

When sending cryptos to another wallet it's important to verify three things:

- What specific type of crypto is being sent?

- Whether or not the other wallet supports that crypto.
- And if you have the correct public key/ address.

For example, you can only send Bitcoin to Bitcoin addresses and you can only send Ether to Ether addresses.

With so many cold storage wallets out on the market it can be daunting trying to figure out which one will suit your specific needs best. What follows is a description of five of the most popular hardware wallets currently in the market.

Top 5 Hardware Wallets for Safe Crypto Storage:

Your best bet is to purchase a wallet directly from the company, off of the official company website, when you can. Avoid resellers listed on eBay and Amazon like the plague. In this way you know you're not getting a used or unofficial clone of the device. As well, should you be purchasing your device online, verify the vendor's URL to ensure that the URL address has a secure socket layer or "https" protocol. Watch out for fake websites pretending to be legit vendors.

1. Trezor.

https://trezor.io/coins/

The Trezor Model T is on the pricey side being sold for $190 US. Most of the time, the Model T is air-gapped, meaning that it isn't physically connected to the Internet. However, if you want to use it, you'll need to plug it into your computer or smart phone with a USB connector. The current model doesn't provide connectivity with iPhones.

Overall, this is one of the simplest and easiest devices to set up and use for cold storage of your cryptos. It also has the advantage of supporting over 1600 coins and tokens, making it the front runner in versatility amongst the five devices discussed.

The Model T has a large, color, touch screen making it easy to use.

Trezor integrates well with the mobile storage device Exodus. This enables investors using a mobile storage device like Exodus to add another layer of protection on their smart phones.

Another option to consider is the Trezor One, which is a cost-conscious alternative to the Model T. It's reasonably priced at $59 US. Sure, you won't get the same display features of the Model T; however, the Trezor One has the same basic features from which you'll still be able to benefit. Unfortunately, some of the more popular emerging coins are not supported by this entry level model. If flexibility is a major concern, then the Model T might be the better option between the two.

2. KeepKey.

https://keepkey.zendesk.com

KeepKey has been around since Shapeshift created it back in 2015. So, it's fully integrated with the Shapeshift global trading platform, thus allowing you to trade cryptos safely and securely.

It has a long, positive track record for being a top-of-the-line cryptocurrency cold storage device. And for $49 US, it's competitively priced. It not only has an unusually large screen for being a compact device, but also comes with many features that make it an even more attractive choice.

Earlier versions of KeepKey did experience a PIN extraction vulnerability. However, most recent devices have been updated with a firmware patch that corrects the problem.

KeepKey allows you to store over 40 coins and tokens. The one drawback for more experienced investors is that this cold storage device doesn't support some of the hot coins in the market. Having an attractive price point makes this device a good option for the novice investor just getting into the crypto market.

3. Ellipal Titan.

https://www.ellipal.com

Ellipal Titan is an air-gapped wallet, which means that you just need to plug the connector into a power source to connect to the Internet. The wallet cannot be connected to devices requiring a USB, WIFI or Bluetooth connection. It can never be physically connected to any other devices or networks. It relies solely on QR code transfer of information.

This is a relatively new wallet in the market. And it tends to be on the pricier side of cold storage options available being sold for $139 US.

The anti-tamper properties of this wallet make it a good choice against physical attacks. Being made of metal components, it's virtually impossible to crack open without physically damaging the contents.

The Titan supports over 7000 assets making it a good choice for the investor looking at building an extensive portfolio of coins and tokens. All blockchains are natively supported, ruling out the reliance on third-party apps.

This wallet also allows you to "stake", or lend out, your coins in order to earn interest off your coins. It integrates well with decentralized finance (DeFi) applications making trading anywhere easier.

4. Coldcard.

https://coldcardwallet.com

The Coldcard Mk3 looks like a glorified calculator and is priced at $120 US. This particular wallet is one of the most secure wallets available. It has an optional duress PIN code used to mask your holdings. It only gives at attacker access to a fake wallet. You also have access to a "brick me" PIN which will destroy the secure element and render your Coldcard worthless should you be under duress. You will require your "seed" words to recover your wallet. Coldcard also shuts down after 13 failed attempts to brute force hack one's way into the wallet. Another security advantage is that the code used to generate the Coldcard wallet is open source, making it easier to verify changes to the main coding.

The biggest drawback is that this wallet only supports Bitcoin. No altcoins are currently supported with this storage device. And since the device has so many layers of security and protection, it becomes more challenging to use.

If you only intend on investing in Bitcoin, then this wallet offers a massive amount of security. It's a great choice should you build a substantial position in Bitcoin.

5. LedgerWallet.

https://www.ledgerwallet.com

Although this hardware wallet company had a solid reputation up until mid 2020, they experienced a setback with a corporate data breech that dumped tens of thousands of emails, phone numbers and addresses onto the Internet. This led to a series of emails and phone calls being sent from scammers to those individuals impacted by the data breech. Fortunately, the device itself has a stellar record against intrusion by hackers.

The Ledger Nano S costs around $75 US. It can keep track of up to 27 coins and 1500 tokens. This device has a storage capacity of 3 to 6 applications depending on the app size. This should only pose a problem if you have a large extensive portfolio of cryptos to manage. Otherwise, this hardware device is a solid choice for novice investors or those requiring a limited storage capacity at an attractive price point.

The Ledger Nano S supports some of the more popular coins like Bitcoin, Ether, XRP, Bitcoin Cash, EOS and Stellar. You have the ability to safely install and uninstall apps on your device to optimize storage space. Another big plus is that "staking" with Ledger is supported with platforms like Tezos, Tron, Cosmos and Algorand.

Ledger integrates well with a host of Web 3.0 wallets like Metamask, which is essential for DeFi.

The Ledger Nano X is $148 US, which comes with a bigger screen, better built quality and Bluetooth connectivity with the Ledger Live app on your mobile phone. The Nano X can store up to 100 applications from a list of over 1500 compatible assets like Bitcoin, Ether, XRP and EOS. This is a great option for the serious crypto investor who is holding a myriad of cryptocurrencies. But for the novice investor the Nano S is a cheaper yet functional alternative.

If you're able to pick up a backup pack, do so, as this will provide you with another layer of security and peace of mind knowing you have a backup wallet. The biggest threat to cold storage devices is actually physically losing the device. Lose the hardware device - lose your coins.

Now that you have an idea as to how you could further protect your crypto holdings, it's time to do a deep dive into how to make crypto purchases in the next chapter.

~

BUYING CRYPTOCURRENCIES

Currently the most common approach to buying and selling cryptocurrencies is through an exchange. Exchanges offer a convenient and relatively safe way for most cryptocurrency investors to access the markets. For an individual wanting to invest in this new asset class, exchanges are a good option.

As time evolves and more and more individuals worldwide access mobile apps for the exchange of cryptos, we'll see a gradual shift towards peer-to-peer transactions. This will likely occur more readily in developing countries where access to financial institutions is limited and the cryptocurrency market is seen as more of a means to exchange value for goods and services being locally produced.

However, for those investors wanting to remain outside of the direct scrutiny of central authorities, this approach may see a higher adoption rate, especially if central authorities try to strictly regulate cryptocurrency decentralized platforms.

Buying Cryptocurrencies on an Exchange:

Step 1: Create a Coinbase Pro, Binance, Kraken or other exchange account.

Sign up online with your preferred exchange by first creating an account with the provider. You'll typically be asked to create a username, strong password and provide an email address like the ProtonMail one you may have created earlier. Once you verify your email address, you'll be able to move to the next step of the account verification process.

This entails first entering your smart phone number and verifying your phone number, usually through a two-factor identification process. All legitimate exchanges compliant with federal guidelines will request you to verify your identity after you've connected your devices. This can be done a number of ways using a combination of government-issued photo ID, date of birth, banking, occupation and residency information. Ensure that you enter all the information required accurately so as to ensure your account won't be frozen should there be a discrepancy.

Step 2: Connect a funding account to the exchange.

Often, you'll be presented with an assortment of funding options such as your bank account, PayPal, wire transfer or a debit card. Using a bank account often provides a more reliable source of funds with faster approval and larger funding amounts. PayPal and debit cards should only be used for small transactions.

Your exchange will then prompt you to select your financial institution from a list of accredited institutions. You'll be asked to login to your financial institution to complete the set-up procedure.

Step 3: Configure the security settings of the exchange account.

This step involves connecting your two-step authentication app to your account and your phone. You'll initially receive a SMS text containing the 6-digit code for connecting the app. Then you'll need to scan the bar code presented to connect your specific phone to the exchange's platform.

Step 4: Verify your identity with an exchange.

When you've connected your devices to the exchange, you're ready to verify your identity, which is the most time-consuming step of the whole process as it requires human verification of any submitted documents. After you've uploaded the documents requested by the exchange, either the exchange will accept them or request additional information.

Step 5: Buy Bitcoin, Ethereum, and other cryptocurrencies.

When your account has been fully approved, you're ready to fund your account. One of the fastest and easiest ways is through your bank account using an e-Transfer. For the very first transaction you may run into a snag while your financial institution verifies the funding request. If you want to be proactive, give the financial institution a call should the transaction come up as being "pending" and ask that it be pushed through. Once the financial institution realizes that this is a legit request, they should quickly honor the transfer. Future e-Transfers should occur seamlessly and quickly.

To purchase a particular cryptocurrency listed on the exchange, just click on the buy/sell tab for the currency you would like to buy. Your order will be sent to the exchange as a market order and executed at the current market price for the coin or token. Once the transaction goes through your purchase will be stored in a specific wallet for that cryptocurrency on your exchange.

For every transaction accredited to your account, you'll want to ensure you record the particulars of each position you're holding in your paper journal.

Keep in mind, that exchanges cannot help you track down funds or correct many user errors due to inattention or incorrect information being posted. This is why it's important to get into the habit of double-checking each financial transaction before hitting the send button.

Step 6: Transfer coins to a hard wallet for offline storage.

To further protect your cryptos, you'll want to transfer your "cloud stored" holdings onto a cold storage hardware device. If you've purchased and received a hardware storage device, it's time to transfer your holdings offline.

After you've taken the time to set up your hardware devices, it's time to transfer your coins to them. On your crypto exchange, click on the receive button. Navigate to the corresponding virtual wallet holding the cryptocurrency you would like to transfer.

You'll then need to plug in your devices to your computer, open the device using the secure password or PIN code you've set up previously and navigate to the Bitcoin or Altcoin app on your device.

You'll be prompted at some point on your computer screen to continue and verify the address for the Bitcoin (or Altcoin) you would like to transfer. Compare the address listed on your computer with that listed on your device. If they match, click the copy button on your computer. Then, on your hardware device download the data file by tapping the "approve" button.

On the crypto exchange go to the specific wallet you'll be transferring your coins from and select the device you would like them to be sent to. Once the transaction is complete, you'll see the crypto transaction listed on your hardware device.

Step 7: How to transfer coins back to an exchange.

To reverse the process of sending cryptos from your hardware device to an exchange or another crypto trader use the send function on your device. Start by opening the hardware device and selecting the send button. Choose the corresponding coin and amount you would like to send from your hardware device.

Now, log into your exchange, go to the accounts section and select the wallet you would like to transfer funds into. Hit the receive button for the wallet in question and copy the address.

Return to your hardware device and paste the copied address into the recipient's field. Choose the coin you would like to send as well as the level of fees you would like to incur. The higher the fees, the faster the transaction will occur. Most investors select just a standard rate of transfer.

Next enter the PIN code on your hardware device and navigate to the coin you would like to transfer back to the exchange. Once the device has been connected and unlocked, you can then verify your transaction before confirming the send request.

Now you can either sell this coin for fiat currency or purchase another cryptocurrency through the exchange.

Peer-to-Peer Transactions:

If you decide to do in person peer-to-peer transactions with your cell phone, you'll probably want to use the QR code generated by the crypto app installed on your phone to share your address in order to complete any transactions. QR codes have been used by the banking industry for years to securely approve payments in stores. The other party can use a mobile phone to scan your code into their crypto wallet. With this code they're able to complete the transaction and transfer the coin to your wallet.

With Bitcoin, each transaction is confirmed by six separate networks before officially taking place. Every 10 minutes, a new block is released into the Bitcoin network and a transaction is then confirmed. Every sale receives a single block confirmation. This just means that the confirmation process may take up to an hour before you'll be able to access and trade or spend your Bitcoins.

Here are some additional tips when looking at doing a face-to-face exchange:

1. Meet in Public:

Trade in public where you feel safe. If possible, go with a family member or someone you trust. Also don't choose a place that's potentially directly linked to you, such as your place of work, local coffee shop or frequently visited establishment. You can never be 100 percent sure of who you're dealing with. Take some extra precautions. It's not unlike meeting someone to transact a sale on Craigslist, Facebook Marketplace or Kijiji.

2. Verify Current Coin or Token Values:

Always check the current value (rate of exchange) of your cryptocurrency online before agreeing to a price for a peer-to-peer trade. Cryptos operate in a free unregulated market with coin prices based solely upon supply and demand. You can charge whatever you want for your coins and conversely be charged whatever the market will bear. This is why it's important to know the current online pricing in the market before committing. Having said this, expect to pay slightly more for your coins as opposed to going through an exchange.

3. Decide on a Payment Method in Advance:

Peer-to-peer purchases can provide you with more payment options versus using an exchange. More often than not, cash will be the most common form of payment. However, you may find a local who'll accept bank transfers. Don't expect to use PayPal or credit cards as these methods can be used to charge back funds.

Hopefully, these insights will give you a greater sense of confidence in dealing with peer-to-peer transactions.

∽

FACTORS AFFECTING A COIN'S PRICE

This particular chapter is geared towards the intermediate investor who would like to take a more active role in their cryptocurrency investing. Although this may be the intent, every novice investor would benefit from the insights being shared. At the very least, it'll provide you with a deep understanding as to those major factors influencing the price of any cryptocurrency. Once you're able to digest the key concepts, you'll be in a better position to find market leaders, analyze their growth potential and make a more rational investment decision based on the merits or positive attributes that can factor into a coin or token's success.

What is Tokenomics?

When evaluating a crypto coin or token, tokenomics is an important criterion to integrate into the analysis process. Tokenomics is short for token economics. It looks at a number of factors that come into play in determining the value of any one coin or token.

Although the term coin and token has been used interchangeably in the crypto space, there are some subtle differences. Coins are cryptocurrencies that are native to their own platform's blockchain. The three most notable coins in circulation are Bitcoin (BTC), Monero (XMR) and the Ethereum network coin Ether (ETH). Coins are used to transfer value, to pay fees on the network and to reward miners when a new block is mined.

Tokens do not have their own native blockchains and may exist on multiple platforms. Instead of being used for a platform's activities that are reserved for coin payments, tokens have unique uses specific to the projects that created them. For example, the Decentraland mana token is burned when digital assets are purchased on the Decentraland marketplace. The term "token burning" refers to the process of permanently removing some tokens from circulation.

The biggest difference between coins and tokens is how they're treated by regulators. Coins function like currencies and as such are designated as currencies under Securities and Exchange Commission (SEC) rules and guidelines. Tokens can have variable functions. They can be issued like stocks in a company. This can create a mountain pf paperwork to be processed by the SEC before any company can issue or trade securities like stocks. Very few cryptocurrency projects have filed the appropriate paperwork to the SEC making this class of digital currency suspect. The SEC has levied heavy fines against several tokens over the past few years as a result. This is why you need to think twice before investing in any tokens that don't have the blessing of the SEC. It's also important to determine the likelihood of any coin or token running into regulatory issues down the road.

To do so, check out the rating for coins and tokens posted by the Crypto Rating Council (http://www.cryptoratingcouncil.com). The Crypto Rating Council is made up of a group of crypto businesses who have focused much of their attention on regulatory compliance with U.S. federal securities laws. The goal of this organization is to make it easier for members to apply the law more consistently and efficiently across digital assets. They have evaluated the regulatory risk of major coins and tokens.

The Crypto Rating Council uses a 5-point rating system based on a set of factual elements that assess each element of the legal test for investment contracts. The rating assessment process is based on both case law and SEC guidance. A rating of 1 out of 5 indicates that the coin or token has few or no characteristics consistent with it being treated as an investment contract and is therefore not a security under SEC guidelines and federal laws. A score of 5 out of 5 means that there is a high correlation to being treated as a security.

By checking out how the coin or token you're considering investing in is being treated as a security or not, you'll be in a better position to assess if the asset might run into future regulatory challenges. Assets that rank high on the 5-point scale run the risk of greater regulatory scrutiny and control, as well as tax implications.

Although you need not have this level of understanding in order to make a small long-term buy and hold investment of one of the top cryptocurrencies, these collective insights become essential when you decide to dive in beyond investing a few hundred bucks. Let's first explore how the price you pay for a crypto is not the same as the real intrinsic value it has.

Price and value are not the same thing in the eyes of a seasoned crypto investor. The price of any coin is determined by Mr. Market. And Mr. Market tends to be moody. He'll be euphoric one moment and assign a high dollar value to a coin during a buying frenzy only to change his mind and panic, dumping coins at any price during a selloff. Price is what you pay. Value is what you get when you look at how useful a coin will be now and into the future.

Twelve Key Factors Affecting the Price of a Coin:

So, what factors have affected the price of a coin the most in the past decade? Here's a snapshot of a dozen of the most important factors to think about that affect coin prices.

1. Popularity.

Ask yourself: How many users could end up adopting the cryptocurrency over time for completing common financial transactions? Transactions could be as simple as the act of buying and selling goods, exchanging property or assets or monitoring the flow of products. The use of digital monetary platforms is on the rise, especially in underdeveloped areas of the world that don't have the same level of widespread financial services as we have in North America. Worldwide adoption of digital currencies is accelerating as the unbanked now have a platform that empowers them to control their financial affairs.

In general, the greater the adoption rate of cryptos world-wide, the greater the demand for certain coins and coin-based networks offering financial services. As popularity for these alternative financial solutions become engrained in a particular society, lives change for the better. This fuels an increase in the adoption rate for a cryptocurrency. And the greater the demand of a fixed supply asset, like most cryptos, the higher the price it can command.

2. Regulations.

How many restrictive regulations are being imposed on the crypto market by regulatory government agencies? The more loopholes and restrictions governments try to impose, the slower the adoption rate and ensuing popularity by the masses. This could conceivably stifle demand and place downward pressure on coin prices.

Fortunately, most developed nations are not moving to severely restrict this asset class. They're moving to enforce tax obligations for traders and investor alike. This collective approach is no different than the tax obligations investors in other asset classes experience.

We all need to be compliant with our country's current tax laws. Avoid trying to hide any realized gains by not reporting taxable transactions. It's always better to be upfront with your investments. I know that this flies in the face of one of the main reasons why a decentralized financial system has come into existence. Many of us are frustrated with the heavy hand of government and financial agencies in getting too personal with our financial data. The only way around this obstacle is to play within the confines of the current tax system and learn how to better protect your financial assets.

This guide will offer some concrete suggestions as to how you can eventually structure your holdings so as to minimize any tax obligations in the future. Once you know what you can and cannot do in the eyes of the law, you'll be in a better position to take advantage of the same legal strategies and loopholes afforded major corporations and hedge funds holding investments.

3. Usefulness.

How useful is a particular cryptocurrency platform in solving real issues that people value in society? Radical changes as to how an industry operates moving forward into the future, has a direct impact on the price a coin can command. Take for example, the rise of Amazon, which has replaced the need for brick-and-mortar shops for selling goods. This was particularly apparent during the COVID-19 pandemic, whereby many local merchants were forced to close their doors - some for forever.

The world saw a definitive shift from in-person shopping to online purchases. As a result, the need for paper money as a medium of exchange has become unnecessary in many cases. This shift from a physical currency to a digital medium is taking place at an alarming rate. The next radical shift underway is moving financial transactions away from a centralized system of digital services like credit and debit cards controlled by financial institutions to peer-to-peer decentralized transactions using cryptocurrency networks.

Not only that but whole industries could be radically changed by implementing features unique to blockchain technology, especially in the financial and business sectors. From an investment point of view, this is an important one to take into consideration. Those businesses capable of using blockchain technology to make permanent lasting change in industries as they become more decentralized and digital will command a higher price for their underlying cryptocurrency.

4. News.

The influence of mainstream media and social media platforms on the pricing of cryptocurrencies in the market cannot be neglected. Positive news from reputable news outlets with a long-standing reputation can bolster trust in the crypto market. The media plays a significant role in how the masses perceive what is taking place in the world of cryptos. Media hype can drive prices skyward, as can trash talk in triggering massive selloffs. This factor becomes a more important consideration as we explore how the media hype can influence when to buy and sell positions.

You'll notice that many of the daily cryptocurrency videos on YouTube play up the hype and price potential of various coins. Take care not to get too caught up in the over-enthusiasm of many of the You Tubers. When I visit video sharing platforms, I focus my attention on educational videos. I look for current documentaries, "how to" videos and thoughtful, well-researched presentations rather than opinion-based talk shows or blurbs. I especially avoid the ones that have presenters who are over the top with enthusiasm, like a Jack Russel dog bouncing off the walls.

The same can be said of any media outlet. The smart investor seeks out information channels that focus on improving one's level of understanding of the financial markets. Ask yourself: Am I learning a new skill, investment strategy or insightful approach that's going to make me a better all-around investor?

5. Whales.

The impact of large investors or whales can cause significant changes in a coin's price. Unloading large quantities of coins into the market at low prices creates a ripple effect on the rest of the market. Often, it's the whale traders who are trying to temporarily manipulate the market in order to try to sell high and buy back in low, thus affecting a coin's volatility.

Over the past decade, we've experienced high price volatility levels in the cryptocurrency space, with coin prices going through the roof only to free fall as market movers cash in their positions. Part of the problem lies in the fact that there has been a lack of institutional support from traditional players like hedge funds, pension funds and major corporations. Many of these institutions take a long-term view or approach to investing preferring to buy and hold investments long-term. The latter part of 2020 saw an increase in the stake institutional investors have in Bitcoin. This will add some stability to the crypto market.

When you're aware of this market manipulation by the whales who are trading their positions, it becomes easier to understand their intentions and come up with an appropriate strategy that takes advantage of the situation. In most case, if you're holding onto a position long-term, it's best to go grab a cup of freshly brewed coffee and kick back and relax. Let the traders do their temporary dance in the markets, while you sip on that delicious nectar of the Gods.

6. Growing pains.

Every new baby experiences growing pains, and the cryptocurrency market has experienced many over the past decade. This market is so new that it has undergone extreme volatility as it works through major hiccups along the way. What has been healthy for this market are the wild swings in valuations from massive bull runs to devastating bear markets. This has been extremely healthy in weeding out many weak cryptocurrency projects while strengthening the best of breed coins. Moving forward these wild fluctuations should diminish as the market consolidates and valuations become more predictable.

As previously mentioned, when institutional investors look to cryptos as a long-term deflationary storage of value, you'll find fewer traders manipulating the markets. This has historically taken place in most markets. As the market matures, best practices evolve so that the market remains robust. When the kinks have been worked out, more retail (do-it-yourself) investors pop into the market with the added confidence that the market will help to build their wealth over time.

7. Supply.

When checking out any coin or token, the first factor you need to verify is the total circulating supply of that coin or token. The larger the supply, the less likely you'll see wide markets swings or manipulation by the whales. This is not unlike a cruise ship, which can navigate in heavy seas more so than the Minnow from Gilligan's Island. Digital currencies with a smaller market cap are affected by the whims of the overall market oscillating between huge gains and dramatic losses.

For example, Dogecoin (DOGE) has a massive supply and relatively stable steady growth pattern. On the flip side, a Yearn Finance's wi-fi token Yearn (YFI) has a small supply. It may be subject to increased volatility. The trade-off is that it may also have greater upside growth potential due to its more limited supply. This is because a cryptocurrency with a market cap of $1 billion has an easier time of doubling compared to one at $10 billion.

Which brings us to an important point. You should focus more on a coin's total market cap rather than its price. Recall that a coin's market cap is calculated by multiplying the current price of the coin multiplied by the total number of coins mined and in circulation. You should also compare coins in terms of percentage changes in growth as opposed to price changes. The raw numbers being displayed for a coin's price don't allow for an accurate comparison of growth between coins. Percentage gains and losses do. Focus on the rate of change. It's a more meaningful metric.

Cryptocurrency market caps are currently loosely grouped into three categories:

1. Large-cap cryptocurrencies: These are coins that exceed $10 billion US, like Bitcoin (BTC) and Ethereum (ETH). They're popular coins with an assortment of different types of investors as they tend to offer a lower risk level as an investment. Both coins have a demonstrated track record for growth, high liquidity and demand popularity.
2. Mid-cap cryptocurrencies: Coins that have a market cap between $1 and $10 billion fall into this category. Coins like Ripple (XRP), Litecoin (LTC) and EOS (EOS) theoretically have more upside potential, but also carry a higher level of investment risk. Some cryptos in this category are displaying the same growth patterns as many mid-cap growth stocks in the stock market, making them good momentum plays.
3. Small-cap cryptocurrencies: The vast majority of coins and tokens fall into the small cap universe, which contain all digital currencies under $1 billion. They're the most volatile, yet potentially the most

lucrative cryptos. Many crypto traders are drawn into this universe as dramatic returns can be generated, not unlike the penny stocks found in the stock investing world.

Also, it may be helpful to compare the number of coins currently in circulation to the total number of coins theoretically available or fully diluted valuation. Most coin systems have a certain number of coins that are locked up by the network for internal projects or still need to be mined. You can quickly check this information about the current market cap out on Coin Market Cap (http://coinmarketcap.com).

Then you can compare this market cap metric to the fully diluted valuation of the coin on Coin Gecko (http://www.coingecko.com). The fully diluted valuation takes into consideration the total theoretical number of coins when you include those in circulation, those tied up and even potentially lost coins.

8. Allocation.

Cryptocurrencies can be created in two ways, by fair launch or by pre-mining. A fair launch occurs when a part of the crypto's community start collectively mining for that coin or token. Bitcoin, Litecoin and Dogecoin all underwent fair coin launches. This being said there are no coin or token allocations for fair launches. Everyone gets a fair shake at mining and acquiring the asset.

Where allocation becomes a decision-making factor is for those coins and tokens that were pre-mined. In this case, the team behind the project allocates a certain number or percentage of coins available to be used by the team. Some of these coins are sold prior to the launch in order to raise capital from venture capital investors for building the network. Also, major network contributors can be rewarded with coins just prior to the launch. Many of the ERC-20 tokens sold on the Ethereum network were sold or allocated this way.

The allocation process happens prior to opening up the network to miners and the general public. The launch is usually done through an Initial Coin Offering (ICO). An ICO functions similar to what takes place in the stock market when a private company is taken public during an Initial Public Offering (IPO) in order to raise corporate capital.

This can pose a problem for you the investor. If the numbers of coins or tokens available through an ICO is small and the number of coins or tokens being allocated is proportionately high, future growth is limited. This becomes even more of a factor when the insiders sell their positions as the coin or token is ramping up and starting to take off during a bull run.

To help you with this assessment, verify how these coins or tokens were allocated by looking up the ICO details you're researching on a website like ICO Drops (http://www.icodrops.com). ICO Drop lists all those coins and tokens that are currently undergoing an active ICO, upcoming ICO's and those ICO's that have recently ended.

9. Distribution.

Once you know how the coins or tokens are being allocated, you can check out how they're actually being distributed by using Blockchain explorers, such as Blockchain.com. Verify if the stated allocations match up with the total supply available listed on the website. You're double checking to ensure that the stated allocations match up closely with the distributed amounts. This step is necessary only for pre-mined coins and tokens.

Once you've done a comparison check for a pre-mined launch, it's also important to look at whether or not there is a fair distribution of coins or tokens across the network. If you're researching an ERC-20 token use Etherscan (http://www.etherscan.io).

Here you can investigate all of the top tokens, charts, statistics, and holders. To check out a particular ERC-20 token, enter its name in the search bar. Once that token's stats come up, scroll down and click on the "Holders" tab. This will provide you with a listing of the top wallets holding the token along with the percentage amount. You may also see wallets that are designated as holding coins or tokens specifically for smart contract use. These allocations tend to be tied up in the network and are usually not readily available for sale.

You'll see tokens being allocated for supporting the network as well as individual wallets of whales holding substantial positions. Again, it's not the raw number of tokens you should focus on but the percentage of the total holdings being controlled by just a few wallets.

If you're researching a Binance defi token, check out BscScan (http://www.bscscan.com) where you can explore and search the Binance blockchain for transactions, prices, and other activities taking place on Binance (BNB). And if you're researching a coin or token that isn't native to Bitcoin or Ethereum, visit the Avalanche Explorer Network (https://explorer.avax.network). Some of the more obscure block explorers can be difficult to use as they tend to hide data that potential investors might use in their decision-making assessment of a coin or token's future potential.

What you're trying to determine is to what degree the coin or token's distributions are inequitable. Are any wallets holding a concerning supply of that coin or token? For example, over one quarter of the supply of Dogecoin is being held in just one wallet. Too many tokens in too few wallets means there's a risk that these whales could dump their crypto on the market causing a huge price swing in the short term.

10. Vesting.

Vesting only applies to pre-mined cryptos where those early benefactors, can opt to sell their holdings at a pre-defined vesting revoke date. This is not unlike what we see in the stock market where corporate executives are often required to hold onto their positions for a pre-defined period of time after their private company goes public.

The vesting process determines how the coins or tokens are expected to be allocated over the coming month and years. It's common to see a portion of pre-mined coins and tokens being locked up and gradually released over time. This increases the confidence of regular token holders that the market won't be flooded by tokens that were allocated to the launch team and private investors.

Usually, these vesting schedules are pretty logical and take place over many years. However, should you see a vesting schedule that has a substantial dump of tokens being released early in the launch phase, this should trigger an alarm. Too many tokens being released for sale all at once or within a short time span can sink the price action of that token in the short term. Avoid coins and tokens where the risk of substantial future market volatility is inevitable.

11. Inflation.

A cryptocurrency is either inflationary or deflationary. Inflation of a crypto causes it to lose purchasing power and its attraction as an investment. If a crypto experiences too much inflation, it can reduce the value of the current coins and tokens already in circulation. Inflation occurs when the supply of cryptos increases over time. Proof-of-stake cryptocurrencies often have some degree of inflation to incentivize validators and delegators on the network, which normally ranges from 5 to 15 percent.

Many decentralized finance tokens use inflation to reward liquidity providers and yield farmers on their respective protocols. These tokens often have very aggressive inflation schedules to keep their annual percentage yields high. Ethereum creator Vitalik Buterin likens these particular defi tokens to the

Federal Reserve's money printer. This is why many advise do not buy them, earn them. In other words, it's better to earn these defi tokens as a liquidity provider or yield farmer than to buy them on an exchange.

If the cryptocurrency is deflationary, the reduction in supply over time increases the value of that crypto. This is why coins like Bitcoin are becoming more valuable. With a limited supply being released over a twenty-year period of time, supply being cut in half every four years and a market cap of 21 million coins, inflationary effects are kept in check.

What makes Bitcoin and several other coins deflationary is accidental loss, which takes actively traded coins out of the supply. For example, Ripple's former CTO may have lost as much as $220 million in Bitcoin because he can't remember the password to his hard drive containing over 7000 BTC. If true, this has diminished the supply of Bitcoin making it more deflationary in nature. When these types of human errors occur, the total supply of Bitcoin in circulation also diminishes.

Some cryptos reduce their supply by "burning" coins or tokens. For example, an upgrade to Ethereum would burn part of the Ether coins used to pay for the network fees. Burning takes coins permanently out of circulation. Even though Ethereum was originally set up to be inflationary with no fixed cap on Ether coins, by burning fees inflation is kept in check. When Ethereum 2.0 kicks in over the next couple of years this could make the coin more deflationary in nature like Bitcoin and drive the price up significantly.

12. Staking.

Staking is the act of locking up a portion of your cryptocurrencies in order to receive rewards, usually in the form of additional coins or tokens. When one stakes their coins as a validator or delegator, the coins are locked up for a period of time. When coins are taken out of circulation, they don't participate in any runs in the market. This often has a positive effect as an investment since fewer coins make their way onto exchanges. As we've already discussed, when supply is tight and demand is high, coin prices rise.

A perfect example of this is with Polkadot (DOT), which has their website listing that 60 percent of the supply has been staked as of early 2021. The tokens are subject to a 28-day unlock period, which is more than adequate time to see significant price changes in the short term. An explosion in price often occurs over several days or a couple of weeks before correcting. This is more than adequate time for non-stakers to capitalize on the positive uptrend.

On the flip side, a coin like Cardano (AKA), which has no staked coins could see a flurry of coins heading onto exchanges during a bull rally as investors try to cash in on the excitement. This has the potential of quickly driving the coin's price down right after a positive rally.

To check out how the level of staking could impact the future price direction of a coin or token, visit the crypto's website. By navigating around the site, you should be able to get a feel for how the coin or token is being allocated, distributed, vested and staked. All of these factors play a role in assessing the merits of any crypto.

Understanding how these twelve factors can influence a coin's price in the short and long-term is an important consideration to take into account when investing actively in cryptocurrencies. But are there other elements that affect a coin's price? Which brings us to look at how coin price is influenced by cycles.

The Cryptocurrency Market Cycle:

All financial markets follow an economic cycle varying in length from 1 to 12 years long, going from contracting to expanding. The cryptocurrency market is relatively young compared to more established financial market like stocks, bonds and precious metals. Being young, it cycles through periods of volatility rising and falling on a more frequent basis.

The current overall trend with the crypto market is that we're seeing a 4-year cycle made up of a 2 to 3-year bull market followed by a 1 to 2-year bear market. The term 'bull" market refers to a market that is expanding and growing an investor's equity. Whereas a "bear" market refers to the opposite - a period of contraction and consolidation with a corresponding decrease in an investor's equity.

The crypto market growth trend can be broken down into four phases, each having psychological stages that investors go through, as follows:

Expansion:

During the expansion phase the market experiences rapid growth. The market as a whole is fueled by optimism that a rally is unfolding. We begin to see more money being poured into the markets as new investors get caught up in the belief that it's time to get fully invested. FIMO begins to rear its ugly head. The Fear Of Missing Out drives up demand for cryptos and with a limited supply of most cryptos in circulation, prices rise dramatically.

Peak:

At some point during the rapid expansion phase, investors get caught up in the buying frenzy. Everyone is in a state of euphoria thinking that they're investment genius's and gloating about how rich they're becoming. You'll see lots of media attention reporting on the new crypto millionaires being created. This overheated and perhaps overpriced market is ripe for a correction. Should you find yourself overexcited about the way the market is heading, it's time to consider taking some money off the table.

Contraction:

During the early part of the contraction phase, many of the big players or whales cash in on what the market has generated. The bull-run is stagnating and showing signs of reversing. Many investors become complacent believing that the correction unfolding is just temporary in nature. The market may oscillate up and down for months before showing a definitive downward trend. At this point, it's too late for many investors who have seen their positions dwindle away. The fear of losing becomes a strong negative catalyst that delays the realization of a loss, which then turns into a more significant loss. Despite substantial losses, many investors will hang onto their positions in the hope that the markets will rally once again. As the bear market becomes a reality, investors panic and desperately dump their remaining holdings for fear of losing everything. During the panic stage, major selloffs are occurring.

Trough:

People are at their lowest level of confidence in the markets. Market sentiment tends to be pessimistic. The cryptocurrency market is at its low point and growth begins to recover. At this point in time many of the unnecessary "dumb money" projects have been killed. Only the stronger real projects supported by "smart money" display any promise of future universal adoption and growth. This consolidation period is essential for any strong market to grow long-term. You need to separate the chafe from the wheat, which can be planted to grow a substantial crypto crop next season. It's during the trough phase that smart investors pump money into well-established cryptos whose prices are at their lowest levels.

What Has Caused the Rise in the Cryptocurrency Market Value?

Keep in mind that markets tend to revert to the mean over time. This means that coin prices whether they're undervalued or overvalued eventually gravitate towards a fair market value. In the case of cryptocurrencies, the fair market value has risen substantially over the past 10 years. This rise in value can be attributed to several factors, such as:

- World-wide access and ease of adoption by those who are underbanked.
- Opposition to central banks and governments who are attempting to control a decentralized peer-to-peer market.
- Utility of each coin in solving real-world problems that in many cases replace third party interventions.
- Improved trust with better security measures for exchanges and digital wallets.
- Fear of inflation with an increasing supply of fiat currency worldwide.
- Greater confidence by consumers in using digital currency platforms.
- Adoption by major corporations, hedge funds and even financial institutions of cryptocurrencies as a deflationary storage of long-term investment value.

Market cycles are a natural part of the evolution of the overall crypto marketplace. When you understand how the crypto market cycles through periods of growth and consolidation, it becomes a lot easier to develop an investment strategy that takes advantage of these normal phases of expansion and contraction.

Another element we need to integrate into any price model for cryptocurrencies is the concept of mining. It has shown to have a direct correlation to the last three market cycles.

Who Are the Miners?

Crypto gets its worth from its scarcity. There are usually a finite number of coins in circulation for any particular crypto. It's not unlike gold or silver which cannot be reproduced at will like paper currencies. Precious metals need to be painstakingly mined, refined and stored. Fortunately, cryptocurrencies are all initially created with a mere digital encoded entry and stored in a virtual ledger. These digital ledgers are stored in various computers around the globe making the network a decentralized platform.

In order for a coin to be created and entered into the marketplace as a digital entry, it has to be "mined" using mathematical algorithms. Every crypto that has come into existence has been mined through that crypto's mining network.

Miners create wealth in the form of new cryptocurrency units being found. The cost to do so for Bitcoin as of late 2020 varies from $12,000 to $15,000 per coin. As more of these units are mined and found, they become scarcer. And as a cryptocurrency becomes scarcer to mine, it becomes more challenging for miners to search for any new blocks originally created at the inception of the cryptocurrency.

Miners are paid a fixed amount for the newly mined crypto units when they are found and added to the blockchain. They also serve as the record guardians for crypto communities. And they receive a variable number of existing units paid by the buyers of coins and tokens. For this reason, mining appeals to the tech savvy entrepreneur who has access to state-of-the art computer hardware to do the mining and a cheap power supply. As you can imagine, miners use large amounts of computing power to verify the integrity, accuracy and safety of the blockchains of data.

Bitcoin for example has a maximum supply of 21 million units. Not all coins were released in 2009. Small quantities of coins are systematically released that miners actively look for on the Internet. The release of new Bitcoins is slowing down every year. Some have predicted that Bitcoin should be all mined out by 2140, at which point the intrinsic value of Bitcoin will be based on the scarcity of the coin along with its popularity by users.

What Are the Effects of Bitcoin Halving's?

A Bitcoin halving event is when the reward for mining Bitcoin transactions is cut in half. These halving's take place every 210,000 blocks of newly released coins, which occurs roughly every four years. The halving also cuts the inflation rate of the coin. And it decreases the rate at which new Bitcoins enter circulation, resulting in miners being paid less for their efforts. The halving event has forced many mom-and-pop shops to close their doors as they're no longer able to compete with the massive mining farms set up by major players. Halving's have occurred:

Halving 1: Nov. 28, 2012

Halving 2: July 9, 2016

Halving 3: May 11, 2020

Halving 4: Expected in May 2024

These events have corresponded to the bull market run-ups that occurred in 2013, 2017 and 2021. Coincidence? Maybe. But I personally don't think so at least for the next cycle. I believe that the markets as a whole will require more time to consolidate to a point that mainstream business and financial institutions embrace cryptocurrencies as a long-term buy-and-hold asset to hold.

From an investment perspective, once a particular market exceeds the trillion-dollar market capitalization level, it is officially recognized as a legitimate asset class. Now that the cryptocurrency market has surpassed that trillion-dollar level, more institutional buyers will be entering the market.

Having an idea as to the various factors that affect a coin's price gives you a better understanding as to what to take into consideration when investing in cryptos. We've now reached the point of drilling down even further in the assessment process for determining the merits of one crypto over another.

～

ASSESSING POTENTIAL INVESTMENT OPPORTUNITIES

It has been the Wild West over the past decade in the cryptocurrency marketplace. Coin and token valuations have skyrocketed through the roof only to plummet as traders cash in their positions taking profits in the process. Most investors in the crypto space who have not experienced the extreme highs and lows of a typical 4-year market cycle have trouble with this level of market volatility.

They'll question themselves, wondering if they've made the right investment decision. This becomes less of a concern when you have a long time horizon for investing in cryptocurrencies since all viable markets cycle through periods of highs and lows. Fortunately, all markets climb upward in price valuations for that asset class over the long haul. If they didn't, investors wouldn't consider investing in a marketplace that guarantees lower returns over time. No matter what market you're investing in as a buy and hold investor, short-term market volatility isn't going to impact your long-term positions.

When market volatility becomes a mitigating factor is when you decide as an investor to become more actively involved in the investment process. You may eventually decide to dabble in timing certain trades, trying to take advantage of mispricing in the crypto marketplace. This is why it's important to have a basic understanding as to what options are available to you down the road as you evolve as an investor. Many of you will start out with the initial goal of becoming buy and hold investors of cryptos. However, as in stock market investing, you can improve your odds of success and potential returns with a little investment knowledge. Let's explore some key factors you should be aware of in assessing any potential investment opportunity outside of the two market leaders Bitcoin and Ethereum.

Investing versus Trading:

As you may surmise, many cryptocurrency buyers and sellers are speculating as opposed to investing. They're focusing on trading cryptos in the short-term using primarily technical charts and indicators to guide them in their decision-making process.

And as previously mentioned, the primary focus of this guide is to give you a solid background in the cryptocurrency investment process. However, it may be helpful to briefly look at both so that you have a more comprehensive understanding of the differences. This'll also help you formulate your own personal investment philosophy for your particular situation.

Investing as opposed to trading has three important distinctions that you should be aware of, namely:

- Timeframe.
- Frequency.
- Objective.

1. Timeframe.

The length of time that you hold onto a position plays an important role into whether or not you're trading an asset class. We often refer to those buy and sell transactions occurring for a particular coin or token that take place within a one-year timeframe as being more aligned with trading. Transactions that take place over a period of years are generally regarded as being investments. This loose definition is in line with what most tax jurisdictions consider to be trades versus investments. And as you'll see in the chapter on tax implications, the time period that you hold onto any position factors into how much tax you could end up paying.

2. Frequency.

How often you buy and sell positions over the course of a year also is a determining factor in assessing whether or not you're trading cryptos or investing in them. Buy and sell transactions made on a regular basis during the year are an obvious indication that you've put on your trader's hat. However, one must be careful as to the timing of these transactions. Disposing of even one position within a one-year time frame may be deemed to be a trade and this applies to bartering, swapping, or gifting coins. When you purchase coins and tokens and hold them over the course of a year before selling, trading, bartering or disposing of the cryptocurrency, in all likelihood you're engaged in an investment process according to most tax authorities.

3. Objective.

The last factor that comes into play in assessing whether you're trading or investing, is the purpose of a transaction. We all start the investment process by purchasing a coin or token. From this point forward, you can head down the path of having placed a trade or taken the investment route. Your intention becomes an important decision-making criterion. If your intent was to quickly profit from a market situation, tax authorities will probably deem that your sell transaction is more in line with a trade. When you contrast this with a typical buy and hold strategy used in many financial markets, the disposition of an asset after a holding period of one year is usually considered to be an investment.

We'll explore each of these factors in greater detail when we look at the tax implications of trading versus investing on your bottom line. What's important to grasp is that the shorter your holding period, the more frequent your buy/sell transactions, and having the intention of turning a quick profit fall into the category of speculative trading.

Fundamental and Technical Analysis:

Assessment criteria can be loosely categorized as belonging to either a group of fundamental indicators or technical indicators. Fundamental factors take an objective look at how certain variables impact a coin or token's price. Fundamental factors like tokenomics, the coin's usefulness, the composition of the development team, the software platform behind the coin and user support can influence price. Many of these variables can be quantitatively analyzed. This provides an objective assessment as to a coin or token's growth potential. For this reason, many hodlers who prefer long-term buy and hold investment strategies spend most of their time focusing on the fundamentals.

We can contrast this approach with the day trader who uses technical analysis and charting programs to guide their buy and sell decisions. Technical analysis zeros in on those subjective variables like buying trends, price movement and investor interest to help predict price movements in the crypto marketplace.

Whether you're a hodler or trader a more eclectic analysis of the market can be derived from a combination of fundamental and technical analysis. For this reason, it's important to understand how each adds value to your decision-making thought process. Ultimately, you want to use as many tools as necessary in order to develop a consistent "edge" in the crypto market. An "edge" is just a higher probability that over time your investment strategies generate more profitable trades than losers.

Also, by using a combination of fundamental and technical indicators in buying and selling positions, you can better time entering and exiting the markets. Ideally, we want to be able to optimize our returns over time. The goal is not to maximize your profitability but rather to move into and out of the marketplace without compromising your initial capital by taking on unnecessary risk.

When it comes to fundamental analysis, we want to look at those tangible, measurable factors that help us assess the current value of the coin or token along with its upside growth potential.

The Impact of Trends on Coin Prices:

It may be helpful to outline just a handful of market trend criteria when assessing any opportunity. Let's start by looking at the following four general trends:

1. The impact of market trends.

One of the best technical indicators you should be familiar with is Bitcoin Dominance. Bitcoin Dominance is the ratio between the market cap of Bitcoin to the rest of the cryptocurrency markets. When the BTC dominance is falling it means that there is a general shift away from Bitcoin to Altcoins. This can translate into higher price valuations for some of the top Altcoins.

Another pattern to look for is when Bitcoin is trading sideways without much price movement. Bitcoin Dominance will remain rangebound for a period of time. When this happens, many traders get bored with Bitcoin and move their money into Altcoins looking for profitable plays. Greed is a strong motivator for many a trader and the Altcoin space has more potential growth plays to capitalize on. Should you decide to diversify your holdings into the Altcoin space, we aware of the potential for higher price volatility.

Keep in mind that Altcoin market valuations tend to follow the Bitcoin market. When Bitcoin rises in price, so does the general Altcoin market. And when Bitcoin's price collapses, so does the price of alt coins. They statistically are highly correlated to each other.

However, based on previous cryptocurrency market cycles, when Bitcoin reaches a market peek and begins its temporary downward journey during the bear market phase, Altcoins continue to peek for a short period of time after Bitcoin's peek. This can be attributed to a subtle shift in the overall market moving out of Bitcoin and into the Altcoin market giving some adept investors the opportunity to profit from the Altcoin surge for a couple of weeks.

2. The impact of institutional investment.

Bitcoin gained solid support in 2021 from large institutional buyers like MicroStrategy, Tesla and Square with more players entering the market every month.

To get a better understanding as to what the market movers are investing in, check out the holdings of the Greyscale Investment Trust, which is the largest institutional holder of cryptocurrencies. Look at the individual funds held within the trust such as the Bitcoin and Ethereum funds to get a graphical sense of where investment money is flowing.

For example, a rising bar graph over time indicates that the trust is bullish on that particular cryptocurrency. When comparing two coins or several side by side, look at the rate of growth as opposed to the raw numbers. The rate of growth, or percentage change over a period of time, gives you a true comparison of money flow into each coin. As already pointed out, the raw numbers on their own can lead to a misleading assessment as to what the money flow trend is telling you.

3. The impact of utility demand.

How a particular coin can be used in society to solve practical and useful problems is another major consideration to take into account. For example, Bitcoin has always been known as a coin that can store and hold value especially during periods of inflation. It's digital gold. It's also a form of value exchange in that goods and services can be bought and sold using the coin. The utility demand for solving problems pales in comparison to its investment demand. Bitcoin's primary usage has shifted from being a medium of exchange to a store of value, not unlike gold.

On the other hand, Ethereum is a programming platform built on the concept of using smart contracts on a developer blockchain to create hands-off solutions to many problems in areas like finance, healthcare, and logistics. Ether, the coin used on the Ethereum network, serves as an exchange of value. The extensive utility demand of smart contract integrations on the Ethereum blockchain network is where this Altcoin will see an increase in demand.

As you can see both Bitcoin and Ether have different uses and advantages that ultimately impact demand. One metric that'll help you quickly assess the growth potential of any cryptocurrency is using a market cap analysis of the growth rate. This is accomplished by comparing the current total market cap for that coin or token and comparing it to the initial coin offering or IPO. You could also select any timeframe that includes at least one entire market cycle for the entire asset class, as in the example below. Here's a 3-step calculation as to how to get a rough estimate of a coin's annual growth rate:

Step 1: Calculate the current total market cap, which is equal to the market price per coin or token multiplied by the total number of coins or tokens in circulation.

For example, Bitcoin's annual average growth rate for the roughly 4-year period from the halving on July 9, 2016 until the most recent halving on May 11, 2020, can be calculated as follows:

Bitcoin's market cap on May 10, 2020 was $160.885 Billion at a coin price of $8756.

Step 2: Calculate the initial public offering cap, which is equal to the launch value per coin or token multiplied by the total number of coins or tokens. You could also use any time period prior to the current total market cap instead. This would give you the growth rate for a specific time period, instead of from inception.

In our example, Bitcoin's market cap on July 10, 2016 was $10.228 Billion at a coin price of $649.

Step 3: Calculate the growth rate, which is equal to the current total cap minus the IPO Cap divided by the IPO Cap. Multiple this value by 100 and divide it by the number of years the coin or token has been in existence to arrive at the annual growth rate. This percentage growth rate approximates an annual average return a coin or token generates.

For our example, the time frame was the recent market cycle of 3 years 10 months or 3.83 years.

The annual growth rate between the most recent halving's was equal to:

(160.885 - 10.228) / 10.228 x 100 / 3.83

This provides us with an approximate annual rate of return of 385 percent.

I don't know about you but that's an enticing growth rate for any asset class. Granted over time the crypto market will generate lower annual returns, however, it won't drop precipitously over the next market cycle or two. If the crypto space evolves like many mature markets such as the stock market, we can expect high rates of return for many well-established cryptocurrencies with a proven track record of utility.

4. The impact of supply.

When the supply of a commodity is limited and demand for it is high, prices tend to rise. This is the case for Bitcoin, which has a fixed supply of 21 million coins that should all be mined by 2140.

With an Altcoin like Ether, the supply doesn't have a hard cap. Should there be an additional release of coins in the future, inflationary downward pressure on the value of the coin is a real possibility. Currently, the circulating supply of Ether is pegged at just under 115 million coins.

What's important to look at is how much of a coin's supply is actually locked up and not in a sellable form. The more a coin's supply is locked up and unable to be readily traded, the higher the price potential of that coin due to its scarcity.

For example, even though Bitcoin is being used by many as a long-term store of value, there's nothing stopping a hodler (a buy and hold investor) from selling his or her holdings. This makes the theoretical sellable supply of Bitcoin high.

Contrast this scenario with Ether. There is a huge demand for Ether to be used in decentralized finance protocols, whereby coins are locked up with an exchange that pays interest on the deposit. A lot of Ether is locked up in smart contracts and as collateral in the DeFi marketplace. This means that the percentage of sellable coins is limited, even more so than Bitcoin. This has a greater impact on supply and the future value of the coin. Keep this in mind, when assessing the merits of one coin over another, as supply is an important consideration.

6 Steps to Assessing Potential Crypto Investments:

The process of assessing the growth potential of any cryptocurrency starts with creating a short list of possible candidates. To do so, you'll want to apply just a handful of specific selection criteria to each opportunity. Once you've identified some coins or tokens that you would like to explore further, you'll then want to look at using both fundamental and technical analysis to help determine when you should enter the market.

In this chapter we're going to use a top-down approach to creating a watchlist of possible investment plays using a six-step evaluation process that delves into:

- Step 1: Does the coin or token have a useful purpose in society?
- Step 2: Is the coin or token built on a technically sound platform?
- Step 3: Is the project backed by a solid team of developers and programmers?
- Step 4: Does the project have lots of positive support by potential users in the crypto community?
- Step 5: Is the coin or token economically active?
- Step 6: Who controls the supply of coins or tokens?

In the following chapter, we'll explore market timing options using a handful of technical indicators. And we'll also integrate several investment rules into the market analysis process that'll help generate more consistent growth plays over time.

Let's jump right into the six steps that'll help you better determine which cryptocurrencies are showing promise as future growth plays.

Step 1: Does the coin or token have a useful purpose in society?

The platform must have a useful purpose. Is the platform useful, beyond just having coins available? Does it meet a need in the marketplace that is currently underserviced? For a coin to take off and gain traction, it must solve a problem. It must also be able to exploit an opportunity or weakness in a particular market. This could be a lack of pre-existing competitors using blockchain applications to solve a specific problem, or it could be the application of blockchain technology that revolutionizes how business will be conducted in the future.

The first step to assessing this aspect, starts with researching the project's whitepaper. The development team will post a detailed proposal for the project, prior to raising any funds for financing it's development. Look at the quality of the proposal. Does it provide a lot of detailed information? Is the proposal well-researched with supporting documents or sources?

You can use the "Profile" section on a site like Messari (https://messari.io) to dive deeper into the history, tokenomics, token allocations and milestone timelines for the project. Although this is a reputable, professional source of insights, the information may be dated. Keep this in mind as you investigate potential prospects to invest in.

Step 2: Is the coin or token built on a technically sound platform?

The platform must be technically sound if users are going to adopt it. How does this project set itself apart from all other similar projects? In other words, what is its unique selling proposition?

To answer these questions, check out the feedback on the social network sites like Twitter and Facebook that are following the project. Look for comments that target or criticize the technical aspects of the platform's development.

Also use Binance (https://research.binance.com) to get a more technical analysis of how the cryptocurrency works.

Ask yourself, why is this project better than the competition? Does the code look technically sound and provide a better solution to any other project the platform is trying to solve?

Look for projects that use open-source code from a popular platform like Ethereum. These projects are less likely to encounter possible coding issues as opposed to closed loop software applications or unknown and untested platforms.

Step 3: Is the project backed by a solid team of developers and programmers?

The platform should be backed by an experienced and extensive team. What is the quality of the development team? Are the developers and programmers known for their innovative concepts and applications? The team should be made up of a core of software engineers and cryptographers who understand blockchain technology. They need to have an established track record or a demonstrated experience that sets them apart.

Once again, a site like Messari can provide you with the names of key founding members. You can jot these down and Google their names to get more detailed information about these individuals. As well, check out their LinkedIn profiles to see what their work experience and track record might be.

Next, go to You Tube and watch the most recent videos interviewing these key players. Just arrange them in chronological order before watching them to get a feel for how the project they're supporting is progressing. To save you some time, watch the videos at 2X speed and take advantage of any timestamps that are posted for the video.

Also, look for support from the cryptography community who is actively engaged in providing feedback and suggestions for modifying the open-source code being developed. Visit the platform's website to see how many contributors and commits the project is generating. With a couple of hundred contributors and several thousand commits, you've got a platform showing traction.

Also, check out activity and posts about the project on some of these specific sites:

- Discord
- Github
- Telegram
- Slack Channel.

Mindshare is an important attribute to see happening in order for a successful project to have any legs and momentum moving forward. These websites and platforms should provide you with those insights.

Step 4: Does the project have lots of positive support by potential users in the crypto community?

The platform must be driven by positive sentiment. Does the community that's following the project's development, sound optimistic and upbeat about the prospects? Is there a lot of chatter on social media platforms indicating a bullish sentiment?

Check out the number of followers on social media platforms. What does Google Trends have to say about the project? With increasing posting on various social media sites, you're apt to see a rise in visibility in the community. If the sentiment is upbeat and encouraging, investors are more likely to support the project financially.

Alternatively, you can use the services of a sentiment analysis tool that'll identify whether what's being said about a given topic is positive, negative or neutral. Most sentiment analysis companies in the crypto space will analyze what's being said on Twitter about a specific crypto by analyzing a hashtag or specific word or phrase. Some investigate what the popular news sources are saying about a cryptocurrency. How people feel about a crypto at any given moment in time is what is going to drive the price for that crypto.

This is a relatively new field in the crypto space with few platforms being able to accurately predict sentiment and its impact on price movements. Most of these services are in their infancy. Tensorcharts.com and the Crypto Fear and Greed Index (https://alternative.me/crypto/fear-and-greed-index/) are some platforms to check out, should you be interested in exploring sentiment analysis further.

Step 5: Is the coin or token economically active?

Verify the market activity to see what volume of coins or tokens are being traded. Many Altcoins have no or little trading volume to mention. You can use platforms like Coin Market Cap (https://coinmarketcap.com) and Coin Gecko (https://coingecko.com) to see what the real 24-hour market dollar volume and price action has been for the crypto. These sites are great for tracking price action and doing your initial research.

Look for the coin being listed on at least one major global exchange and having a significant volume of activity. If it isn't you could find yourself paying a premium for the coin since the order books may not be as deep.

Proceed with caution for any ERC-20 token that is traded almost exclusively on decentralized exchanges like Uniswap as DEXs don't have any listing criteria or requirements.

You can also use a crypto coin calendar that lists major events to help you better assess timing opportunities. An announcement of an Altcoin being listed on a major new exchange can boost the price. One such coin calendar to use can be accessed at Coin Market Calendar (https://coinmarketcal.com/en/).

Once you've established that the cryptocurrency has an economic pulse, you're in a better position to determine if you have a potential investment opportunity.

Step 6: Who controls the supply of coins or tokens?

Another factor to take into consideration is the number of coins or tokens that are under the control of the founders. Ideally, there should be a very limited supply going to the founding members with the vast majority being made available to the general public. This ensures that you won't be negatively impacted by a coin dump by the founding members in the future. You can use either Messari or Binance to get some basic information. Then, double check these sources against insights you may be able to get from the website ICO Drops (https://icodrops.com), which lists all active, upcoming and ended Initial Coin Offerings. This site provides detailed information about all fundraising projects related to coins and tokens in the cryptocurrency marketplace.

Assessing the potential profitability of any coin or token requires that you apply a number of assessment criteria in the analysis. The 6-step process outlined in this chapter should have you asking the right questions before investing in any one opportunity. You should now have a much better idea as to how to select winners and eliminate most of the losers. You've now been empowered even more in developing your "winning edge" in the markets.

∽

10

ENTRY STRATEGIES FOR BUYING CRYPTOS

In this chapter, we're going to explore two fundamental aspects of acquiring cryptocurrencies taking into account how to effectively time the market so as to optimize your positions. Using a top-down approach, we'll first delve into several crypto acquisition approaches for building your portfolio over time. After you have a better idea as to possible ways to add to your positions, we'll dive deeper into tools you can use to better time moving into and out of the market. You won't be able to consistently time market tops and bottoms. No investor or trader has been able to do so. However, through technical analysis there are certain patterns of behavior you can use to help you be more adept.

In order to build a sizeable position in any asset class it's helpful to approach your investing with two goals in mind:

1. Systematically save to invest.
2. Make that initial investment long-term.

There's nothing quite like making your first crypto acquisition, knowing that over time the funds you've allocated for that initial investment will probably generate a significant return when held long-term.

1. Save to Invest.

The challenge that faces many investors is the inability to take advantage of investment opportunities as they present themselves. You may find yourself currently in this situation, where you've been presented with a super opportunity, yet you're cash strapped.

Unfortunately, very few people place saving as the #1 financial priority for the household. But the truth of the matter is, if you don't have any savings set aside, you cannot invest. If you cannot invest, you dash any hopes of becoming financially free and building the lifestyle you've always dreamt about.

Start today by looking at saving as being a positive active process and not a passive activity. Saving to invest opens up new possibilities. Those possibilities allow you to look forward to working towards realizing your dreams.

Get into the mindset of always paying yourself first. Make your saving process as automatic and disciplined as possible. Automate the process by regularly transferring your earned income into a dedicated savings account earmarked for investing. And you should be disciplined in your approach by using that money to only invest in appreciating assets or your financial education through books, programs, seminars or coaching.

As well, learn to live below your means but within your needs. You need not deprive yourself of those opportunities that create lasting memories; however, being tempted by impulsive purchases or giving into instant gratification won't get you to a point of financial freedom any time soon. By having a frugal approach to spending you create a more positive saving routine for yourself. There's some truth to the notion of short-term pain equating to long-term gain.

Now that you've made saving a priority in your household, it may also help to make a subtle mental shift. Rather than save money in a low interest-bearing account with a typical bank, why not move that cash immediately onto a cryptocurrency exchange? This habit change accomplishes two things. It moves your hard-earned cash onto an exchange. Once the funds arrive, you can quickly allocate them for a cryptocurrency purchase when the time is right. And secondly, any funds invested have a higher probability of generating a significant return. With current saving account interest rates being almost non-existent, this is a tempting option to consider. It's an approach my wife and I have been successfully using for some time now.

2. Your First Crypto Investment.

Whether you're investing in cryptos, stocks, bonds or another asset class, your first investment should try to target the market leader for that asset class. A market leader is an entity that has a proven track record of performing above the market average for that asset class. In the cryptocurrency world the market leader is Bitcoin. It is best-of-breed amongst its competitors and has demonstrated consistent growth over a lengthy time period. It is one of the most accessible coins to purchase using a variety of fiat currencies.

If you're new to cryptocurrencies and/or have a limited amount of capital, your first crypto investment should be in this crypto market leader. Bitcoin is by far the most widely established and accepted store of digital wealth on a global scale. This coin has been more resistant to major corrections producing an annual growth rate of just under 200 percent for the past decade. That $500 initial investment could be worth substantially more in 10 years' time, which brings us to how you should treat this initial investment.

Your first crypto investment in Bitcoin should be hodled. In other words, hold onto your position long term, preferably for decades until you need to use the asset as collateral for another investment or major purchase. Your initial Bitcoin purchase almost becomes a "buy and forget it" position. With Bitcoin generating above average returns compared to any other asset class, it makes sense to let your initial position go through a couple of crypto market cycles before tapping into its accumulated value. And when you do need to use the asset in the future, it's best to use it as collateral rather than cash in a significant portion and have to pay taxes on the disposition.

Building Your Crypto Portfolio:

Before we explore timing your entry into a cryptocurrency market, there are three common approaches to building a sizeable position with any cryptocurrency that you should be aware of, namely:

1. Lump sum investments.
2. Scaling in thirds.
3. Dollar cost averaging.

Each has its merits and downsides. Let's quickly explore each approach now.

1. Lump sum investment.

One of the most common approaches to investing is to allocate funds to a specific investment project when your savings have reached a certain threshold. You may decide in advance that as soon as you have saved $X that you invest $X into a particular position. This approach works well when you want to build a sizeable position in any one cryptocurrency regardless of what the overall market is doing. It's an easy-to-adopt approach when you're planning on using a buy and hold long-term strategy. This investment approach makes sense for our current market situation whereby most crypto investors are optimistic that valuations will rise significantly for years to come for most of the top coins in the marketplace.

2. Scaling in thirds.

This is a more tactical approach to establishing a position in one particular cryptocurrency or the crypto market as a whole. The premise is that you would allocate 1/3 of your investment capital into a project, wait a period of time to see if you could buy in at a discount and then allocate another 1/3 to the project. Finally, you would wait to see how the markets react over a period of days or weeks to see if there was another buy-in opportunity.

This strategy works extremely well in a down trending market, whereby you're able to purchase coins or tokens at lower and lower prices as the market trends lower. With an anticipated bear market expected in late 2022 and into 2023, this investment approach makes a lot of sense.

3. Dollar Cost Averaging.

With dollar cost averaging, you're investing a certain amount of capital at specific intervals. Often these intervals correspond to when you have savings available for investment purposes. So, month end allocations are a common scenario.

The idea behind dollar cost averaging is to set aside a certain amount of your savings for investment purposes. When you can automate the process, it becomes one less stumbling block in the investment process. This strategy works well when you want to build a sizeable position over time for a particular cryptocurrency and you're not interested in trying to time the market. The obvious downside is that you could end up paying a lot more for your position. However, it does work well when markets are relatively neutral since slight movements in price will average out over time.

This approach struggles to provide the adept investor, during periods of high market volatility, with optimal pricing for the acquisitions. By scheduling a specific date with Mr. Market as to when you'll invest, you're letting Mr. Market decide the price you'll pay. You'll need to weigh how much you're willing to monitor crypto price movements in the short term with investing for the long haul.

Which brings us to the topic of how do you better time moving into and out of the markets. This is where technical analysis comes into play. By knowing how to analyze investor behaviour, you can better time your entry into and exit from your positions.

What is Technical Analysis?

Technical analysis looks at price movements over time with the help of graphing tools. One of the most commonly used graphing systems is the candlestick charting approach, which was created by the Japanese rice merchant Homma Munchisa 300 years ago. Many of the patterns and terminologies outlined in his 1755 book "The Fountain of Gold - The Three Monkey Record of Money", are still used by expert traders today. Homma understood that emotions fuel any given market, and these emotions show up in fairly consistent patterns of behavior. These buy and sell patterns of behavior can be graphed and analyzed giving the trader valuable insights into how the market might react moving forward into the future.

Fast forward to the 1970's and the adoption of candlestick charting in Western markets was underway. Technical analysis plays a significant factor in the cryptocurrency marketplace, alongside some of the fundamental factors previously discussed in chapter 9.

Technical analysis focuses almost exclusively on price action as it relates to the volume of sales, magnitude and direction of the price movement, and evolving patterns or trends. Pumps and dumps are caused by the irrational actions of investors holding a coin or token. How much emphasis you place on using fundamentals and technicals will be based on the type of investing you'll be doing. The more you look at timing your entry into and exit from the crypto marketplace, the more important technical analysis will play in your decision-making process. Technical analysis plays a dominant role for short-term trades; whereas fundamental analysis becomes more of a factor with long-term buy and hold investments.

As outlined in the previous chapter, at a minimum, you'll want to narrow down your selection of potential coins and tokens to invest in based first on solid fundamental indicators. Once you've identified a crypto with upside potential based on fundamental metrics, you can now apply some technical indicators to the mix to better time your buy/ sell transactions.

Most technical analysis involves the use of candlestick charts whereby trading activity is graphically represented on each chart. Each candlestick gives you a snapshot of the trading activity within a given unit of time. For example, if you have the chart set for one day, each candlestick represents the trading activity for that coin or token over the course of 24 hours.

Making Sense of Candlestick Charts:

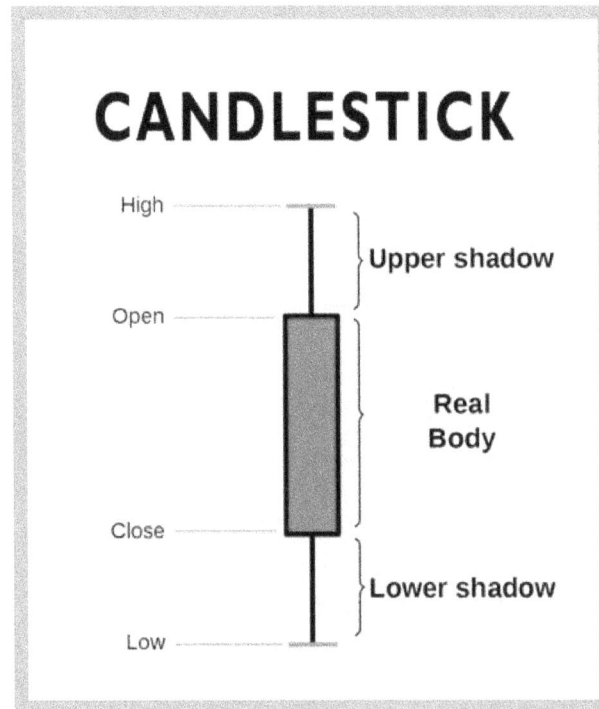

There are two basic types of candlesticks to be aware of. A green candle means the prices went up over that period of time and a red candle indicates that the overall price dropped. Each candlestick has a body and a wick. The body is the thicker part of the candle. The bottom edge of a green candle indicates the opening price of the coin or token with the upper edge signaling the closing price for the time frame. For the red candlestick the upper edge represents the opening price, while the lower edge is the close. When the body is short, trading took place within a narrow price range. A long body indicates that the price moved significantly to the upside or downside depending on the body's color.

The wicks on the candle denote the highest and lowest prices for that trading timeframe. The wicks are useful for indicating when investors are taking profits or buying the dip. A long wick on the bottom often indicates that traders are buying the dip. While a long upper wick usually indicates that traders are selling their positions.

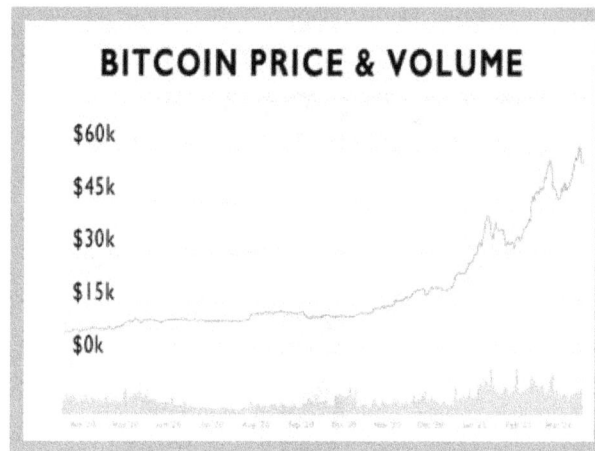

1. Volume.

To really get a handle on price predictions you must also factor in trading volume. Trading volume is often represented by a bar chart along the bottom axis of the overall chart. Green bars indicate that there were more buyers than sellers in the market for a given time period. While a red bar indicates the opposite; more sellers were active.

As a general rule of thumb, you want to be trading in a marketplace that has lots of trade volume. Low volume exchanges often lead to increased price volatility. You may end up paying more for your transactions as a result. Volume is the first technical indicator to verify when buying some hot Altcoin on a shady cryptocurrency exchange.

Volume is used by many traders to confirm a price trend. Just because your coin price is dropping doesn't mean that you should bale on that coin. If the volume is also dropping over time for the coin, this may signal that the downtrend is not very strong despite what the price action may be indicating. The bulls may be waiting for volume to drop off before plowing more money into that particular coin or token. The same holds true for a rising price on low volume. Expect to see a strong price reversal at some point in time should volume diminish.

2. Charting Trends.

Technical traders look for three primary chart trends:

- Support.
- Resistance
- Price Patterns.

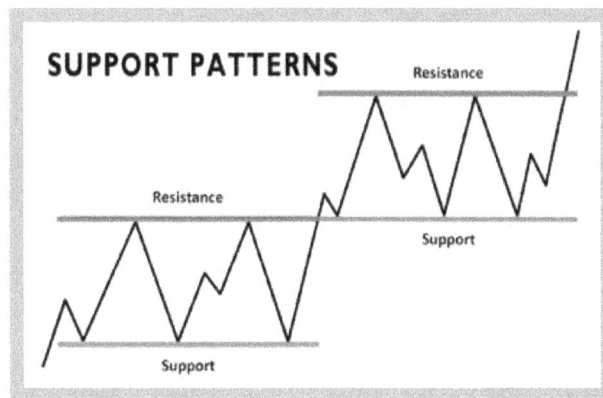

Support refers to the lower limit as to where traders think the price will go. Resistance refers to the upper limit as to where a coin's price may climb to. The most common way to determine support and resistance levels is to draw two straight lines. The support line will be drawn along the most prominent bottom prices. And the resistance line will be drawn along the various price tops. This band can give you a sense of how much volatility the market might experience going forward, along with the direction the price is moving. Support and resistance lines tend to correspond to psychologically comfortable price points like even hundreds or thousands. This helps to assess when you might sell or buy a position.

Price patterns are used by professional traders across a multitude of asset classes. When used in conjunction with trading volume, you'll be better able to assess if the pattern is strong or weak. For example, high transaction volume over a few days with a slight decrease in coin price can signal an eventual sell-off. When you contrast the same situation with a low volume scenario, it may signal a reconsolidation and potential upswing in price movement, especially if the previous time period showed a steady upward trajectory.

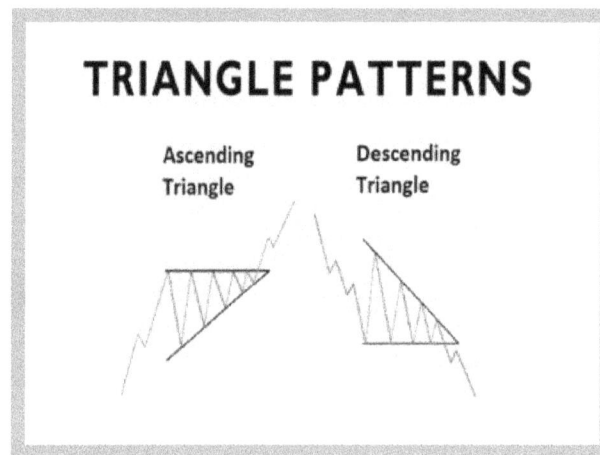

One of the most reliable patterns as a predictor of future price movements is the triangle pattern. An ascending pattern has the support line angled upwards in the direction of an upward price movement breakout. The descending pattern shows a resistance line that is angled downwards and often indicates a downward price correction for a coin. The left side of the triangular wedge can often be used to predict how much the price will move to the upside or downside. The amount of price movement will move up or down based on about the same amount as the widest part of the wedge. The percentage change in the wedge tends to be to the same degree to which price will go to the upside or downside.

When getting involved in technical analysis as a novice or intermediate investor there's no need to spend money on specialized technical indicators. Free indicators that have a proven track record will be more than enough to build a robust technical analysis trading strategy.

4 Key Technical Indicators to Use:

The top four technical indicators you should be aware of should you decide to eventually trade cryptocurrencies are:

1. Moving Averages.
2. MACD.
3. RSI.
4. Bollinger Bands.

These four indicators are commonly used in the stock and options market, which means that they have a proven track record when placed in the hands of a seasoned investor or trader.

1. Moving Averages.

Moving average indicators draw the average price of a coin or token over a given period of time. Exponential moving averages or EMAs are commonly used in technical analysis trading. They place greater weight or emphasis on the most recent time period for the block of time being used in the analysis. For example, a 50-day EMA places greater importance on the time just leading up to present day as opposed to 48 or 50 days out. The 50-day EMA reacts faster to price changes than a 50-day Simple Moving Average, which uses an arithmetic scale as opposed to algorithmic one.

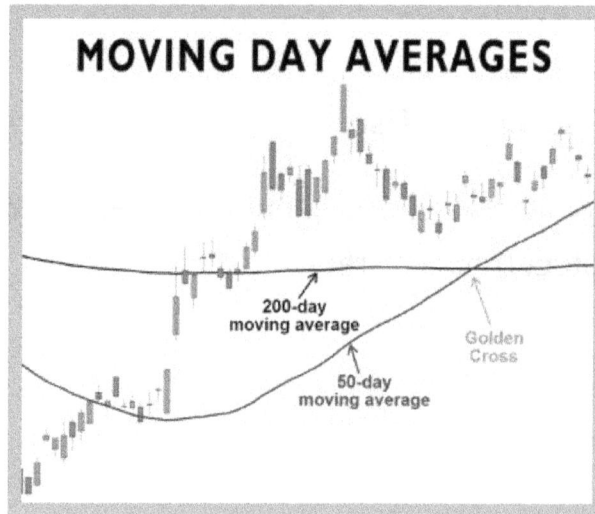

MOVING DAY AVERAGES

200-day
moving average

Golden
Cross

50-day
moving average

Some of the most popular EMAs are the 200-day, 50-day and 20-day time periods.

The 200-day EMA can indicate if the price for that cryptocurrency is within a fair market value range for the coin or token. The 50-day EMA is often used in conjunction with the 200-day EMA.

When the 50-day EMA crosses below the 200-day EMA, this often signals a downturn in the market for that coin or token. This is known as a death cross. And when the 50-day EMA crosses over the 200-day EMA from down below, this is a golden cross. It signals many green days ahead.

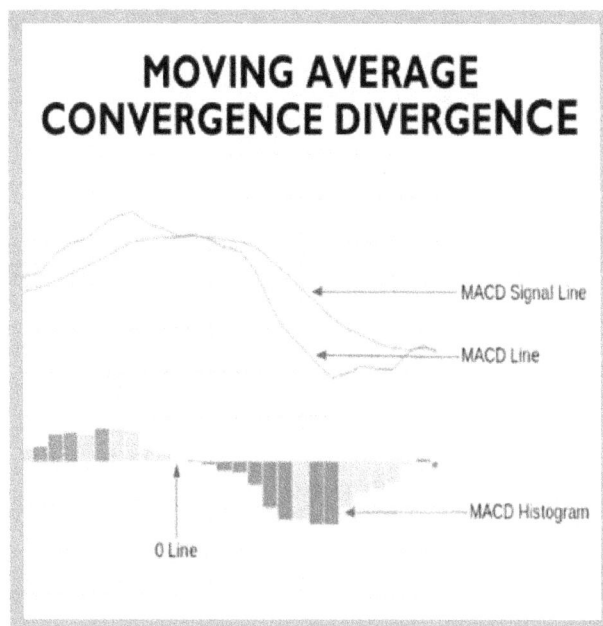

MOVING AVERAGE CONVERGENCE DIVERGENCE

MACD Signal Line

MACD Line

MACD Histogram

0 Line

2. MACD.

The MACD or Moving Average Convergence Divergence is a popular momentum indicator that helps determine when a trend has ended or begun and may reverse direction.

This technical indicator uses two moving average lines and a zero line. The solid black line is called the MACD line and the slower moving red or dotted line is the signal line. When the two moving average lines are far apart that signals that price volatility is low. The closer the lines are together, the higher the price volatility.

When the MACD line crosses above the signal line and the zero line this indicates a positive trend in the market. I prefer looking at a histogram representation of the indicator to graphically tell me when a trend is reversing. When the histogram shifts direction either above or below the zero line, this signals a change in market direction in the coming hours or days. The default setting for the MACD is 12, 26, 9. I like to use a more sensitive setting of 8, 17, 9. You may wish to do the same.

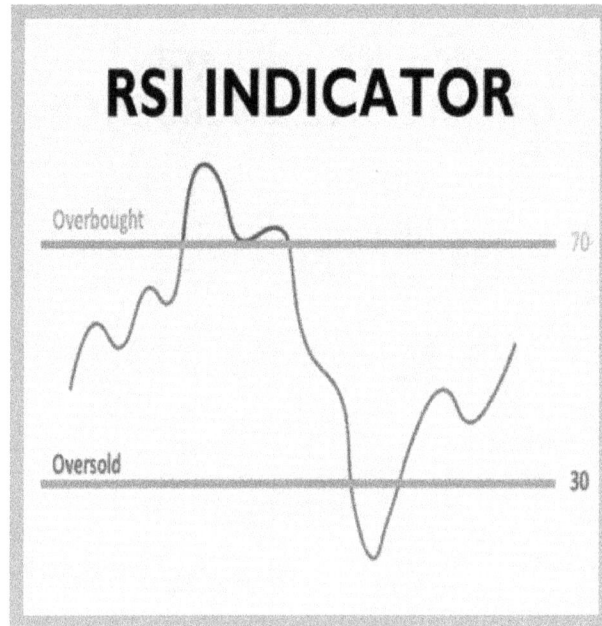

RSI INDICATOR

3. RSI.

The other popular indictor is the relative strength index or RSI which helps to determine if a coin or token has been oversold or overbought by investors. The RSI is an oscillator that moves between 0 and 100. When the RSI rises above 70 or 80, it's a signal that the coin is overbought, and money may begin to flow out of the coin causing a price decline. On the flip side, when the RSI falls below 30 or 20, it's a signal that the coin is oversold, and investors may begin to buy the crypto causing the price to rise.

This particular indicator works best with individual coins and tokens, as opposed to the market as a whole, and with a short-term time frame such as a few weeks. It's therefore a useful tool for helping you move into and out of the crypto markets. Coins with a rising RSI above 50 and below 80, fall into our sweet spot for potential growth candidates.

4. Bollinger Bands.

This is like the MACD in that it's used to measure market volatility. However, in contrast to the MACD, the wider the bands are the more price volatility there is for that particular coin or token. As a general rule of thumb, you'll want to buy when there is low price volatility and sell when there is high volatility assuming that price has gone to the upside during that volatile period.

Using these four technical indicators in tandem should give you enough information to be able to place an appropriate buy/sell order. Take your time learning how to use these indicators. With experience, you'll eventually build a solid investing trading strategy that can be applied to periodic short-term trades and longer-term investments.

Timing Tips:

If you're like most cryptocurrency investors, you'll want to allocate a portion of your overall crypto portfolio for investment in Altcoins. By diversifying your portfolio, you can not only take advantage of coins and tokens having price momentum on their side but also price shifts caused by investors moving between Bitcoin and popular Altcoins.

Altcoins become more attractive when Bitcoin is trading sideways. Investors pull money out of Bitcoin and into Altcoins that show some upside promise. To capitalize on this phenomenon, you can use two additional technical indicators specific to cryptocurrencies to help assess this trend.

The first technical indicator to verify is the Bitcoin dominance or BTC.D Index Chart (https://www.tradingview.com/symbols/CRYPTOCAP-BTC.D/). We briefly touched on this indicator in chapter 9. Look for steadily declining rates from 70 to 60 percent and lower. This usually indicates that investors are moving money out of Bitcoin and into Altcoins. When Bitcoin dominance drops below 50 percent, it usually signals a price surge in some of the top Altcoins. This means money has poured into Altcoins and they may rebound well during a bull run. Historically big drops in Bitcoin dominance have lasted 1-2 weeks giving one plenty of time to exit any Altcoins being propelled higher before the trend starts to reverse.

The second indicator to use in assessing how well your positions are doing in the crypto marketplace is to verify the Altcoin versus Bitcoin value. Using a tool like the ETHBTC Crypto Chart (https://www.tradingview.com/symbols/ETHBTC/) will give you a better appreciation as to how Ether is doing in relation to Bitcoin. Use this or similar tools to see how your Altcoin is rising in value relative to other cryptos in the crypto space. Having this metric enables you to assess whether or not you need to move some of your holdings from a position of relative weakness to one of strength.

Granted these timing tips are more in tune with what you would expect an actively engaged investor or trader to monitor but they do provide you with insights as to how you might exit your positions. If you're familiar with the options market for stocks, Bitcoin acts like a call option in which volatility is an advantage, not a disadvantage for knowledgeable investors. By being able to recognize market timing patterns you're empowering yourself to potentially take advantage of these position plays should you so choose.

~

11

OPTIMIZING LONG-TERM RETURNS

In this chapter we're going to explore how to generate a passive income stream from hodling your cryptos. As well, we'll look at how to use cryptos as collateral for a loan, which could be used to fund a major purchase in the future. Let's start by making the case for hodling.

Bitcoin's Unique Position:

The only time you should sell an asset is if know it will be impaired losing significant value over time and you can't finance it to buy the next asset. Bitcoin is a limited supply digital asset that is being used as a global means of storing value long-term. We currently do not have an alternative asset class showing the same degree of strength and advantages in a global landscape. Stocks, bonds, precious metals and other commodities have limitations. Seasoned investors always strive to move their wealth from weaker assets to stronger ones. This is what is transpiring with Bitcoin. Many institutional investors have begun moving a portion of their overall investment portfolios into cryptocurrencies, with Bitcoin being the digital currency of choice right now.

So as an individual retail investor, why would you trade this strong asset class for a weaker one? This simple argument provides a compelling reason as to why you should hold onto any Bitcoin acquisitions well into the future. If you have a long investment horizon, then hodling Bitcoin and popular Altcoins makes sense. No need to even cash in your positions when you need fiat currency as cryptocurrencies can be used as collateral. You may be able to structure your crypto investments in such a way as to only have to liquidate a fraction of your total holdings in order to meet any financing obligations.

With Bitcoin in particular, if you plan on hodling it forever, you do have a couple of options available to you for accessing your accumulated wealth. You can lend out your Bitcoin, which is known as staking, and be paid monthly interest as a lender. And you can use your Bitcoin holdings as collateral for a loan that could be used to purchase a large ticket item like a real estate investment or starting a systematized online business from the comfort of your home.

Let's take a look at how you could lend out your coins with the goal of generating additional returns to be used to further augment your coin positions or used to fund your desired lifestyle. Although Bitcoin has evolved as the go-to crypto for storing value and has shown itself to work well when you intend to hodle long-term, this investment approach equally applies to some of the more popular coins.

In order to delve deeper into the lending process, we'll want to explore how staking came into existence and where its headed in the future. To best understand where the concept of staking originated, we need to touch on two notions - proof of work and proof of stake.

Proof of Work Consensus:

As we've already explored, decentralized cryptocurrencies like Bitcoin and Ethereum run off a publicly managed ledger of balances known as the blockchain with no one entity having control over it. This ledger is maintained by miners who are rewarded for maintaining the blockchain network and for finding new blocks to be added to the blockchain. Mining is a sort of competition where powerful computers try to guess the solution to a mathematical question. Whoever finds the solution first, earns the right to write the next page of transactions, also known as a block into the ledger. With mining, the more powerful the computer you use, the higher your probability of winning since the computer can generate more guesses per second.

Mining's technical term is "proof of work", because by displaying the right solution, you've demonstrated proof that the work was done. As there is no other way to get to the solution, except by using computing power to constantly work at trying to guess it, once consensus is reached as to who gets to update the ledger a new block is brought into existence on the blockchain network. The proof of work consensus mechanism is a reliable and secure means of verifying the ledger; however, it's also very resource intensive. Running all of these mining supercomputers for the purpose of maintaining a decentralized platform and mining new blocks uses vast amounts of energy.

Proof of Stake Consensus:

This is an alternative approach to mining that's gaining in popularity amongst cryptocurrency developers and programmers. Instead of trying to win a contest for generating new blocks, people will stake actual coins. A simple explanation as to how it works is that you would deposit or "stake" funds in the form of coins or tokens on a network computer known as a "node". Once your stake is in place, you take part in the contest of which node will get to "forge" the next block. Stakers forge blocks, they don't mine them.

The winner of the randomized staking contest is selected by taking into consideration several factors, such as:

- How many coins or tokens are being staked?
- For how long have the coins been staked?
- How the implementation of randomization ensures no one entity will gain a monopoly over the forging?

Whoever wins the forging contest, is rewarded in coins for their contribution to the network.

Some of the popular coins currently using proof of stake are Tezos, Cosmos and Cardano. Each coin has different rules as to how it calculates and distributes rewards.

Of note, is that Ethereum's proof of work blockchain network will shift to a proof of stake consensus system over the next few years. In December of 2020, a new Ethereum 2.0 proof of stake blockchain called the "Beacon chain" was set up. It currently runs alongside the original Ethereum 1.0 blockchain.

In order to join as a "validator" for Ethereum 2.0, stakers need to lock up 32 Ether as collateral. Doing so will earn one access to staking rewards. There's no way to lock up more than 32 Ether on a single node, so if a staker wants to increase their coin reward, they have to set up multiple nodes with 32 Ether each. In a few years Ethereum 2.0 will be fully deployed merging with Ethereum 1.0 in the process. This event known as the "docking" will happen somewhere around 2022 or early 2023. From this point on, Ethereum will become a proof of stake network. Only after the docking occurs will you be able to withdraw your staked Ether and coin rewards.

This passive investment approach to earning additional returns on your Ether is primarily beneficial for long-term Ethereum holders who have sizeable positions as 32 Ether are required in order to be eligible for staking rewards. The amount of Ether awarded to stakers is going to be a percentage of the newly created Ether. This means that the more validators the network has, the smaller the proportion of reward one would receive.

Imagine having a pie with a fixed size. The more validators you have wanting a piece of the pie the smaller the slice of the action. For example, if 1 million Ether are staked, the maximum annual reward that each staker could reach is 18.10 percent. If 3 million Ether were staked, this would drop to 10.45 percent.

As you can see, becoming an Ethereum staker has some limitations. On top of this, each day, only 900 new validators are allowed on board. This means that only 900 new nodes will be created every 24 hours. There's currently a pretty long waiting list for becoming an Ethereum validator. Each validator will require some technical knowledge, a dedicated computer and of course 32 Ether to get started. These constraints create a barrier to entry that most investors will shy away from.

So, how does the regular Joe take advantage of earning staking rewards? There are two approaches to consider. The first is by staking through a cryptocurrency exchange. The second is by joining a staking pool.

The easiest way for a non tech savvy person to stake is on a cryptocurrency exchange offering staking options. Certain exchanges allow you to use coins you already hold on the exchange, even if you're holding a small amount. The exchange charges a small fee for the service. This completely eliminates the hassle of running your own validator. However, you do have to forfeit control over your coins on most exchanges. As in the case of Ether coins, depending on the exchange, you may be able to claim your staking rewards immediately and not have to wait until Ethereum 2.0 reaches the docking phase.

The second option for staking your coins is to join a staking pool. Just like mining pools, whereby a group of like-minded miners pool expertise and hardware resources, staking pools attempt to obtain a higher chance at forging the next block. You can stake smaller amounts of Ether since all of the funds are pooled together.

Unfortunately, with so many crypto scams popping up everywhere in the market, this is one popular target by scam artists claiming to run a legit staking pool. Please ensure that you do your due diligence about the pool. Ample research into the reliability of its validators, pool fees, size of the pool, user reviews, customer support and access to private keys should be addressed before investing.

What Staking Strategy Should You Consider?

As you can see thus far, staking helps you to earn an additional stream of income from being a proof of stake validator. The approach with Ether described above gives you an idea as to one way the staking process can be used to generate additional returns. However, there are other players in the cryptocurrency space that do offer a similar passive income opportunity for your cryptocurrency holdings.

What is interesting to note is that when you do stake your coins on any of the popular staking platforms, you're usually paid in the cryptocurrency you'll be staking. This means that over time, you benefit from any coin price appreciation on both your original stake and the interest or reward paid to you.

Here a few options for you to check out down the road as your holdings grow over time. This is by no means an exhaustive list. It's included here to illustrate the power of lending out your coins when you're a hodler.

1. NEXO.

NEXO is a both a global lender of loans as well as an interest provider for stakers. Based in Switzerland they provide high interest savings accounts with returns as high as 8 percent per annum. They accept Euros and stable coin deposits. Interest is paid daily with no long-term commitments, which is an attractive feature since most banks lock up your funds for a pre-determined time period and pay almost nothing in interest.

2. Cardano.

Staking Cardano's ADA generates a passive income stream on a weekly basis, whereby your coins are not locked up for an entire year or longer as we saw with Ethereum 2.0. It has an attractive yield of just over 5 percent.

3. BlockFi.

BlockFi allows you to not only stake your Bitcoin and Ether to earn passive income, but you can obtain loans backed by your cryptocurrency holdings to finance other projects. BlockFi also compounds interest earned and they pay out in Bitcoin or Ether. BlockFi also has a similar yield to Cardano at roughly 5 percent per annum.

4. Polkadot.

Polkadot is another platform offering staking options. Being relatively new to the staking game, interest rates have been unusually high. Over time, Polkadot should see staking returns drop from their current level of over 10 percent to closer to 6 percent.

5. Celsius.

The Celsius network allows you to earn interest on your crypto and borrow against it. The network has completed more than 160,000 coin loan trades. They've also distributed more than $3 million in interest payments. Celsius is one of the fastest growing lending platforms globally. They too provide an attractive interest rate of just over 6 percent for Bitcoin or Ethereum deposits.

Check out the most popular staking platforms on StakingRewards.com (https://www.stakingrewards.com) for a more up-to-date analysis of coins and tokens you could conceivably lend out. They list more than 180 yield-bearing assets in addition to the top staking providers and top lending platforms.

What Sort of Potential Returns Are We Talking About?

Assuming that you're able to generate a modest return of 5 percent from staking your cryptocurrencies, you would need only a $250,000 commitment to generate approximately $1000 in passive income each month. And should you be able to grow your crypto investment over the next decade to $500,000, this would generate a nice passive income stream of $2000 per month.

You would not only benefit from an income stream that could offset many of your monthly expenses, but you also benefit from any continued price appreciation in your holdings. Even a $20,000 stake would bring in an extra grand each year, just by lending out your coins. If you're hodling your way to retirement, why not consider staking a portion of your holdings and generate another attractive income stream?

What about Getting Loans?

Most cryptocurrency lending platforms offer both an opportunity to earn interest on cryptos deposited on the platform, as well as obtain affordable loans using your cryptos as collateral. As your crypto portfolio grows over time, you may be wondering how you could access the collateral built up to fund other major projects while retaining control over the underlying asset?

When you have grown your cryptocurrency portfolio to have a sizeable monetary value, you can use this asset as collateral for an appreciating asset like real estate or a systematized business.

What's attractive with many investors who decide to use their cryptocurrency as collateral for a loan is that it's easier to obtain a loan even if you have a poor credit rating. Traditional lenders, like the "banksters", are cautious about lending funds to individuals with a dubious credit history. However, many lending platforms operating in the crypto world are primarily concerned with whether or not they have access to the underlying asset.

There are a number of established and emerging loan platforms coming onto the crypto scene. One such platform to consider is NEXO.

NEXO Loans - A Market Leader:

NEXO is a subsidiary of the banking giant Credissimo, which was launched in 2007 and is based in Switzerland. The NEXO cryptocurrency platform was launched in 2017 providing global access to crypto-backed loans. The platform has over 300,000 users with more than $700 million in process transactions. NEXO provides loans in more than 200 countries and 45 different currencies making it a world leader in the crypto lending sphere.

NEXO has its own token. The token offers security features that may not otherwise be accessible on the platform. The token is an asset-backed, dividend-paying token with holders getting 30 percent dividends based on NEXO's profits. The dividends are paid out periodically and proportionately based on how much NEXO an investor holds.

These dividends are paid out in BTC, ETH, NEXO or a USD stable coin.

NEXO is a utility token that offers an interest discount when you pay back your loan using the NEXO token. The company also encourages investors using the NEXO token by offering discounts on the loan interest, access to higher lending limits and access to instant financing based upon the valuation of the token.

NEXO is an ERC-20 token that was issued on the Ethereum blockchain with a total supply of 1 billion tokens of which 525 million were sold to qualified investors. Besides being utility tokens, they are fully compliant with SEC rules around securities making them desirable for qualified investors in accordance with all applicable laws.

Any loans issued are pretty straight-forward. You must first sign up for a NEXO account, then you'll need to deposit crypto assets to your insured and secure NEXO account. Once you complete the customer verification process or KYC (know you customer) documentation, you'll be issued a line of credit instantly with no credit checks. Within the website, you'll be able to see how much of a loan you can obtain based on your initial deposit. Funds being loaned are deposited into your bank account or on a debit card, often within the same day. The amount being loaned will be no more than 50 percent of the total amount of assets you've pledged. You can pay your loan in full, with no penalties; otherwise, you'll typically make monthly repayments in either fiat currency or crypto.

NEXO also has a mobile app, frequently asked questions tool and customer service support that makes your experience with the overall platform streamlined and easy-to-use. This is a great lending platform for those who have experience in crypto and understand how loans work.

The company is a market leader in terms of lending and staking platforms; however, they're not the only consideration. Other lending platforms to check out on your own are:

- Celsius
- BlockFi
- Salt
- Aave, and
- Crypto.com

Paying Back Your Loan:

You may be asking yourself: How do I pay off the loan? Will I need to sell the underlying asset that I purchased with the loan at some future point in time?

The simple answer is "no". As your loan comes due, you could always take out another loan from the same financial institution or another to pay off the old loan with the new. You would roll your debt obligation forward, thus eliminating the need to pay off the loan.

Granted, you would still be on the hook for the typical monthly interest payments that you would have to fund. This would be something you would need to determine in advance. You would need to weigh the pros and cons of using your current earned income, investment income from other sources like stock dividends and option premiums or selling a portion of your cryptocurrency portfolio in order to cover your interest payments.

You could also borrow a little more than you need for your asset purchase against your Bitcoin or another popular Altcoin. If you're able to obtain favorable interest rates, this may provide a solution for funding all or a part of your monthly interest payment obligation.

Should you borrow against your cryptos to buy real estate property in the United States, the interest expense is probably tax-deductible. This is something to verify with a tax specialist.

With a cryptocurrency like Bitcoin being both a good storage of value long-term as well as an appreciating asset, you can use it as collateral for your loan. Since Bitcoin's track record has been stellar when you look at its growth potential historically over the past decade, you could conceivably end up owning an asset that doubles or triples in value over the life of the loan.

This means that if you've pledged $400,000 as collateral for a $200,000 loan for a real estate investment, as your loan comes up for renewal the value of the underlying security could have doubled or tripled in value. You could be sitting on $800,000 or $1,200,000 of Bitcoin. Your debt-to-equity ratio has gone from being 50 percent to under 25 percent, an attractive proposition for any lending institution.

Right now, interest rates offered by many decentralized finance platforms like BlockFi are high coming in at approximately 10 percent for a loan-to-value ratio of 50 percent and as low as 4.5 percent for a loan-to-value ratio of 20 percent over a 12-month period. However, as Bitcoin use as a financial asset gains greater credibility, it will be seen by more and more financial institutions as a preferred asset class for securing collateralized loans. This means that in the not-to-distant future loan interest rates will be slashed. You'll be able to borrow against your Bitcoin at very favorable rates.

If you're considering obtaining a loan in order to purchase more cryptocurrencies, beware. This is known as buying on margin, in which you're using an exchange's or broker's money. If your Bitcoin drops significantly in price, you may be required to post more collateral such as more USD or Bitcoin. This shouldn't pose a problem if you borrow less than 20 percent of your pledged Bitcoin. A margin call shouldn't be triggered unless the coin's price drops close to 80 percent. However, most seasoned crypto investors would advise against borrowing on margin unless you have a deep understanding of the investment process and downside risk.

Now that you have a better idea as to how hodling your cryptos can translate into not only long-term gains, but also generate a monthly income stream or fund major projects without touching your capital, let's look at two exit strategy approaches should you plan on taking a more active role with your investments.

~

12

EXIT STRATEGIES

Let's explore a couple of exit strategies for your cryptocurrency holdings. Once you have an understanding as to how these various exit strategies might apply to your particular investment philosophy, you'll be in a more confident decision-making position.

But before we delve deeper into the two exit strategies, we need to address what to do when the markets get really heated and you want to take profits as soon as possible. Following this we'll look at the "three pillar approach" strategy that focuses on locking in any short-term gains during any bull market run-up and re-positioning yourself for the next buy-in opportunity when the bears take control of the market. And finally, we'll explore the "hybrid approach" exit strategy whereby a portion of your portfolio will be designated for hodling while another portion systematically tries to capture big market moves.

What Is an Exit Strategy?

An exit strategy is used to limit losses and capture gains. It involves following a set of predetermined rules or criteria. The hardest part of exiting when you're going to take a loss is the emotional turmoil it creates. We tend to hold onto losing positions longer than necessary. This is where a pre-defined exit strategy comes in. You never know when the markets will reach a market top. Therefore, you need to periodically take profits on the way up and on the way down, should you decide to take on a more active role with your crypto investments.

The first approach we'll explore is setting multiple milestones that'll trigger a sell order. This is known as the three-pillar approach as it uses multiple criteria to guide you in your decision-making process. The second approach focuses on using a combination of strategies that'll capture long-term gains along with short-term price swings in the market.

Once you decide on how you'll exit, the next step is to determine at what specific price point. These dollar value thresholds should be pre-determined and recorded in your journal along with the initial investment value.

By periodically taking money off the table, you avoid severe losses and are able to buy back in when cryptos are at a discount. This model works well when you've stopped actively pumping large sums of money into the crypto market and you're looking at optimizing the returns of your overall portfolio. You're able to sidestep major corrections by systematically moving your gains into cash in anticipation of market corrections or to fund current projects.

Market versus Limit Orders:

We've previously touched on the concept of market versus limit orders, but it's worth mentioning again in a different context. As you know there are two basic types of orders you can place in order to buy and sell cryptos. They are the "market" order and the "limit" order.

Most investors place market orders when they buy and sell cryptocurrencies. These orders are fulfilled quickly at the current market price the coin or token is trading at. However, you do have the option of buying and selling your cryptos at a specific price point. These are limit orders. They limit the price you're willing to spend or receive in exchange for your coins. These orders are only executed at the limit price.

Most cryptocurrency trading platforms allow you to set a limit order for your sell price of your cryptocurrency. Under normal market conditions a limit order is only triggered when the crypto's price hits that target price. When selecting your specific price exit points, don't use round number points like $4000. Use a number like $3993 instead.

The reason for this is in case a whole slew of other sellers have the same sell point as you do. There's no guarantee that your sell limit order will be executed at your desired exit point. Volatility in the markets could cause the overall market to jump past your limit price. This may occur if no or not enough buyers on the other end are willing to accept your limit price. Market dynamics can intervene, and you may not be able to exit your position as planned. This has happened to me in heated markets when I've placed a "round" limit order. I now place limit orders that are slightly less than the psychologically popular exit points. Two psychologically popular numbers are numbers ending in 0 or 5.

5 Steps to Exiting Positions when Markets Are Heated:

As you know the cryptocurrency marketplace can be extremely volatile with wild price fluctuations and huge volume demand on exchanges. Higher than normal demand can temporarily shut down even the biggest exchanges as they grapple to keep up with fulfilling orders. And with increased demand, transaction fees can go through the roof when trying to exit the market at a specific price point. Ultimately, you may not be able to cash in a position at the price point you desire or have to pay exorbitant transaction fees to get it done.

With this scenario in mind, it may be helpful to establish an exit strategy that has a higher probability of protecting your gains. Doing nothing and allowing the markets to dictate what transpires will in all likelihood result in lower returns. Taking a proactive approach involves several steps. Let's assume that over time you've built up a sizeable position in various popular cryptocurrencies and you would not only like to protect your gains but do so without hitting too many brick walls and obstacles in the process of cashing out. Here's a 5-step process to follow:

Step 1: Move your holdings onto cold storage wallets you control 100 percent.

When you start out investing in cryptos, you may decide that it's not worth the time, effort or money to invest in a cold storage wallet for your holdings. This perception will shift when your crypto holdings blossom and grow to become a significant amount. When you place your coins and tokens on a wallet you control, then you can choose which exchange to use for liquidating a portion of your portfolio. Having your cryptos on a cold storage wallet not only provides an added layer of protection for your assets but also gives you flexibility as to where you'll cash in positions. If your go-to exchange goes down due to high volume, being able to move your crypto from your cold storage wallet to another exchange is a work-around solution.

Also, most of the top wallets allow you to manually set the transaction fees you would ideally like to pay for moving your coins or tokens from your wallet to an exchange. There's no guarantee that your request will be honored but at least you'll have some degree of control over the fees ultimately charged. This dovetails nicely into the next step.

Step 2: Set up several crypto exchange accounts.

Once your crypto holdings grow to a significant monetary value, set up several popular crypto exchange accounts that trade your particular coins and tokens, if you haven't done so already. The reason for this is to be able to use the exchange having the highest degree of liquidity for cashing in your coins and tokens when you want to take money off the table during a hot market. Having most if not all of your coins and tokens on a cold storage device allows you to move your holding onto any exchange you've previously set up.

Ensure you have enough cryptocurrency on the exchange to cover any inflated transaction fees. First, determine which currency you'll need to have on hand to pay for transferring your tokens. If you have Ethereum tokens, be prepared to dish out several hundred dollars in fees per Ether when things get heated and you're determined to cash in your holdings. For Binance tokens, try to have at least $20 worth of BNB tokens on hand.

Step 3: Test each exchange with a very small transaction.

Rather than being caught off guard fumbling around trying to figure out how each exchange is going to handle your withdrawal requests; get a feel for the entire process and any future challenges you may encounter by doing a test run. This'll not only eliminate potentially frustrating circumstances, but you'll also have greater confidence in your ability having already executed a complete withdrawal. Just ensure that you meet the minimum withdrawals rules most exchanges have set up and are aware of the amount of transaction fees being assessed for different withdrawal amounts.

Step 4: Set up a couple of banking options on each exchange.

If you end up wanting to move a significant amount of fiat currency held on a particular exchange into your bank account, you may run into some problems. By moving smaller amounts of funds to two or three bank accounts you won't trigger a red flag whereby the transaction is declined due to suspicious activity, which brings us to the next step.

Step 5: Inform your financial institution that you'll be making a significant cash transaction soon.

By calling your bank and letting them know that you'll be making a significant deposit in the upcoming days or week, they'll be apprised of what is about to transpire. This should decrease the probability the bank will freeze your account for suspicious activity. All financial institutions have a fiduciary responsibility to report any cash transactions above $10K to the federal government in compliance with anti-laundering laws. Ensure that you're not the subject of an in-depth investigation by being proactive.

Now that you have a better idea as to what could transpire when you want to liquidate a substantial position in a hot market, it's time to explore a couple of approaches for managing your holdings.

The Three Pillar Approach:

Time to take a look at a pure market timing exit strategy that takes into account several criteria or triggers. The assumption being made is that you are looking at taking money off the table and locking in your crypto profits periodically during the bull market run-up phase of the crypto market cycle. One of the first questions you'll need to address is: Overall, what realistic return do you want?

A popular, conservative model is to work towards achieving a 10x overall return from your portfolio each crypto cycle. Historically since the inception of Bitcoin, a crypto cycle lasts approximately 4 years. Many popular coins have seen a ten-fold price increase from the bottom of a market cycle to the top. No guarantees here as to future returns but given the past performance of the markets it is a possible outcome. You may wish to dial back on your expectations based on at what point you've actually entered the current cycle. Once you know what your overall objective will be, it's time to look at the 3 pillars that'll trigger the sale of your positions. These are Timeframe, Bitcoin price and Altcoin prices.

The key to these three pillars is that the pillar which triggers the sale of positions takes precedence over the others. For example, if the price of Bitcoin reaches a certain threshold triggering a sell action, this takes priority over the time period or pricing in the Altcoin market. And should your timeframe expectation as to when you'll take money off the table arrive before any price targets, you follow that particular trigger.

Your first task is to set up your sell triggers and the criteria by which you'll exit the market moving into a cash position. Start by setting at least 3 exit "targets" for each pillar. This means you'll have a minimum of 9 exit rules in place over the next cycle. Remember, having a set of pre-defined rules for moving into and out of the market is crucial to your success.

For example, establish 3 times whereby you sell 25% of your entire portfolio, with 25% kept in the market long-term. Or you could establish 7 times whereby you sell 10% of your portfolio with 30% kept in the market long-term. Personally, I like the three-target approach as it requires less time to manage.

1. Timeframe.

First, determine when along the crypto cycle you'll take profits. When do you expect the tops to arrive based on what the experts are saying and what the technical charts of the market cycle are predicting? Ask yourself, is the cycle going to be 4 or 5 years? How similar or different is the current cycle from other bull/bear market cycles for crypto? And, at what point are we at in the current cycle?

A typical bull market runup lasts 2 to 3 years, which is followed by an aggressive bear market lasting 1 to 2 years before starting its upward trend again. Each successive bull market has attained new market highs over the previous cycle.

With this in mind, establish a *timeframe* for when you'll take profits, such as November 2021 to June 2022. You could conceivably start taking profits early in November 2021 and fully exit in June of the following year.

2. Bitcoin Price.

First, determine at which price you think Bitcoin will hit a top. Establish both low and high expectations to establish a *range*. For example, using a range of $75K to $120K, you could conceivably start selling your first portion at $75K per Bitcoin. Your last portion would be sold when Bitcoin reaches $120K.

3. Altcoin Prices.

Choose your two biggest Altcoin holdings and determine at which price point you believe each coin will top out at. As with the Bitcoin price, select a low and high expectation that'll give you a price range to work with. For example, if you're holding Ether and you believe it will reach $3000 on the low end and $6000 on the upper end during the crypto cycle, then your range for this first coin becomes $3000 to $6000. Start selling your first portion at $3000 and your last at $6000. Do the same for your second largest holding.

Note: I've used round numbers for illustrative purposes. When you do exit any position with a limit order avoid setting the limit price with psychologically round numbers. Use odd numbers like $2993 and $5989.

You've now established the exact points in both time and price that'll trigger a sell action. Let's take a look at how this exit strategy might unfold in the following example:

1. Sell 25% of your total portfolio:

   On November 1, 2021

   Or if Bitcoin hits $74,993

   Or if Ether hits $2993 or Litecoin hits $391

2. Sell 25% of your total portfolio:

   On March 1, 2022

   Or if Bitcoin hits $99,993

   Or if Ether hits $4493 or Litecoin hits $447

3. Sell 25% of your total portfolio:

On July 1, 2022

Or if Bitcoin hits $119,989

Or if Ether hits $5989 or Litecoin hits $489

4. Let 25% of your portfolio ride the tide through the next bear market cycle, while you establish your entry and exit strategies for the next crypto market cycle.

As you can see each sell action is theoretically independent of each pillar. For example, if your first sell trigger happens to be Bitcoin reaching $74,993 next week, your next sell trigger might be that of reaching a specific target date a month later and your third might occur another week after that when ETH reaches $4493.

Or you could see ETH reaching $2993 next week, followed by a $4493 trigger a few weeks later, followed by a specific timeframe date of July 1, 2022. As you can see having three interrelated pillars working for you in helping you protect your gains and minimize your losses is key to your investment success. It's the execution of this or a similar plan that will guarantee your long-term success in the cryptocurrency arena.

This approach works well when you're scaling out of your crypto investments. With a smaller capital investment, you may wish to establish just 3 exit targets, instead of 4, that'll allow you to scale out of your positions based on the size of each holding.

The Hybrid Approach:

We've touched on both a buy and hold approach to investing, as well as scaling out of the market when certain exit pillars are reached. Another popular model to follow when managing your crypto portfolio is a hybrid combination of the first two. The overall goals of this approach look at:

- Establishing a core position of crypto positions that'll be held indefinitely.
- Scaling out of a portion of your positions at various stages during the bull market run-up.
- Swing trading a small portion of your portfolio when the market experiences periodic corrections. Or investing in speculative upcoming tokens that have upside growth potential.

Here's how this approach is structured:

You would set aside 50 percent of your portfolio to be held long-term with a minimum time horizon of at least 4 years, preferably indefinitely until retirement approaches. A minimum time frame of at least 4 years allows you to work through an entire crypto market cycle and capitalize on the gains generated during the bull market phase.

Let's assume that you've entered the crypto market relatively early before or during the bull run. Here's how things might unfold. You would allocate 20 percent of the portfolio to be sold when profits reach twice the original investment. It's never wrong to periodically take money off the table for other investments or projects. You could even re-enter the market several months later should an investment opportunity present itself.

You would designate another 20 percent of your portfolio to be sold when profits reach four times the original investment. This allows a small portion of your portfolio to be cashed out when significant gains have been made. In effect, you're scaling out of the market so as to preserve some of your original capital and capture gains in the process.

You would commit up to 10 percent of the portfolio for either swing trading or for speculative investments. This small amount of your total original holdings would be held in cash waiting for either a significant market correction or you could also invest speculatively in upcoming coins and tokens that may show significant gains a month or even a year down the road.

This hybrid approach appeals to those active investors who would like to dabble in trading cryptos with a small portion of their overall crypto portfolio but done so only during major market corrections. It also appeals to those investors willing to spend time researching potential growth plays with upcoming coins and tokens.

This approach won't suit the novice investor just getting into the cryptocurrency marketplace. This is because it requires a higher level of understanding of the cryptocurrency investment process along with some hands-on experience working with various assessment tools and platforms. Even at that, should you purchase most of your cryptocurrencies mid-way through the bull run, you'll need to lower your return expectations and exit the market based on a tighter timeframe.

Calculate the Net Return of Any Exit Decision:

Whatever exit strategy you decide to implement, you should always determine what the net return of your investment decision will be. Your net return should take into account factors like:

- transaction fees associated with selling or disposing of your coin or token.
- exchange withdrawal fees when you move positions off an exchange.
- capital gains tax obligations you'll pay on your annual tax return.
- business taxes you may be required to pay.

Once you understand the full implications of your decision, you'll be in a better position to make the appropriate adjustments to your exit strategy, if need be, to mitigate the effects of withdrawal fees and tax obligations. And this brings us to a discussion about just that in the next chapter where we'll address what the potential tax liabilities might be, based on the exit strategy you employ.

～

13

TAX IMPLICATIONS?

Tax Compliance:

Since I'm not a certified public account, I'm unable to provide you with specific recommendations regarding your tax liabilities. You should consult a CPA to determine what your tax liabilities might be. What follows are some general guidelines pertaining to your potential tax liabilities and what you might expect to see unfold for your particular situation.

Tax avoidance is perfectly legal; however, tax evasion is not. The strategies outlined focus 100 percent on keeping more money in your pockets using legal methods as opposed to trying to cheat the taxman from his portion of any gains. Your goal should be to reduce your tax burden and optimize your holdings for preferential tax treatment.

First, buying or holding cryptos is not a taxable event. The only event that is not taxable is when you take fiat currency and purchase a cryptocurrency. This means that all other events are potentially taxable depending on your local tax laws. Most jurisdictions worldwide consider the selling and exchanging of cryptos to trigger a taxable event. And depending on the circumstances, you'll either pay capital gains taxes on a portion of the gains or income tax on 100 percent.

Start by estimating how much money you expect to make in cryptos in the current tax year. Then, as the year unfolds focus on keeping any taxable events to a minimum. Ideally, you should be "hodling" your crypto and simply adding to your positions over time. When you do need to cash out some of your crypto, it's at this point in time that you'll trigger a taxable event.

More often than not, cryptocurrency investors who opt to hold onto their positions for long periods of time will be subject to a capital gains tax on the gains they've made. These gains are based on the difference between one's acquisition price and the disposal price. Long-term buy and hold investors pay income tax on a portion of the difference once they sell their holdings. They can also claim any losses against current or future capital gains should they decide to sell their holdings below the acquisition price.

Many countries use a 50 percent tax rate for capital gains generated from investments held longer than 1 year. You'll pay income tax on 50 percent of the gains you've made over the course of the year. In the United States the amount of capital gains tax you'll pay is based on your taxable income. A single filer earning under $40,000 would pay no long-term capital gains if the total tax liability falls under the $40,000 threshold. Single filers making between $40,001 and $441,450 would be assessed a 15 percent tax rate on any capital gains. This is where the majority of single filers fall. If you're married and filing jointly, you'll pay a 15% tax should your total household income fall between $80,001 and $496,600.

What Triggers a Taxable Event?

Where it gets complicated in the eyes of taxation law is with investors who "appear" to be engaged in the "trading" of cryptocurrencies. This could be as a result of:

- Day or swing trading, whereby you're frequently moving into and out of positions in the crypto market.
- Trading or swapping one cryptocurrency for another.
- Paying for goods and services with crypto.
- Proceeds generated from mining crypto.
- Interest received from decentralized finance accounts.
- Getting paid as an employee or independent contractor in Bitcoins.
- Gambling with crypto.

These are all taxable events and treated as income tax under the income tax act.

Let's go a little further in-depth as to what specific criteria the government uses to assess whether you're investing or trading in cryptocurrencies.

They use five key factors in their assessment process as to whether a taxpayer's gains are from income or capital, as follows:

1. The frequency of the transactions.
2. The duration of the holdings.
3. The intention to acquire the securities for resale at a profit.
4. The nature and quantity of the securities.
5. The time spent on the activities.

The more frequently you buy and sell cryptocurrencies, the more likely the taxman is going to deem that you're a trader as opposed to an investor. If you're day trading or doing frequent swing trades (selling high - buying low), you'll be more likely to be classified as a trader. All traders are assumed to be in the business of buying and selling securities for profit and any gains are treated as business income.

However, for many in the cryptocurrency space, buying and holding onto coins occurs on an infrequent basis. They may choose to hold onto a particular holding for years before cashing in. This type of behavior is common among investors who focus on long-term capital appreciation as opposed to moving into and out of the market on price swings. The taxman is more than likely to treat this buy and hold tax scenario as capital gains.

Although the intention to make a profit is important, it's not sufficient to establish that you're operating a business since investors and traders want to both make a profit. This factor needs to be taken into account with the previous two. If your intent is to hold onto the investment for over a year as a long-term holding, then this more closely aligns with it being a capital gains scenario.

As to the nature of your activity, should you habitually engage in an activity capable of producing a profit, this more closely aligns with carrying on a trade or business, even if you have a full-time job or occupation elsewhere. This is an important assessment you'll need to take into consideration.

For example, if you have a job that creates a taxable income of $80,000 per annum and you have taxable gains from cryptocurrency sales of $8,000, it's less likely the taxman will deem this to be a side business taxing you accordingly. Contrast this with a student or retiree who both have taxable incomes amounting to $12,000. An $8000 crypto tax liability could be interpreted as coming from business income, even though no formal business has been set up. Granted the tax liability from these two scenarios is not carved in stone. It's used here to underscore the importance of assessing all those factors that could make a material difference to your tax liability.

Finally, the more time you spend on the activity of studying the crypto market and learning about cryptocurrency investing, the more likely you're engaged in a business activity. When you're spending 20+ hours on trading activity, research and studying, the taxman could make the logical assumption that this is not a passive investment vehicle. This daily devotion sets off alarm signals that you're engaged in a business activity.

As a side note, if you know that you'll be taxed on 100% of your gains like a small business would, then it makes sense to claim any business-related expenses even though you're not a licensed small business entity. Just like a small business owner, you're entitled to make reasonable claims against your income with appropriate deductions related to conducting your "business".

These include, but are not limited to:

- Office space rental, which could be a dedicated room in your home.
- Utility costs.
- Internet service fees.
- Computer hardware.
- Office supplies.
- Cold storage wallets.
- Security software.
- Mobile phone service.
- Accounting software.
- Professional development costs.

As you can see, all is not lost when you do have to pay tax on 100% of your gains. You'll be able to offset your income with any legitimate expenses incurred. Hence, the reason why you'll want to keep meticulous records for the taxman.

Records You're Expected to Keep.

Now that you have a better understanding as to how to better assess your particular situation, it's time to put some proactive steps in place so you're 100 percent compliant in the eyes of the law. Here are the different kinds of records you're expected to maintain:

- Transaction dates for your acquisitions and dispositions.
- Receipts of purchase and transfer of crypto.
- The fair market value of the cryptocurrency at the time of the transaction.
- A description of the transaction and the cryptocurrency address of the other party.
- The accounting and legal costs incurred for your transactions.
- The exchange records.
- Digital wallet records and cryptocurrency addresses.
- Software costs related to managing your taxes.

How Can I Track My Tax Liabilities?

Tax calculations can be a nightmare. Making sense of how to handle all of the various transactions from a tax point of view can be overwhelming and time consuming. Since trying to make sense of which events are taxable and at what level, it literally pays to use a software tool that'll help you keep track of all potentially taxable transactions. The top four software tools to consider are:

1. CryptoTrader.tax

CryptoTrader by Coin Ledger is geared for traders and investors alike in the US market. However, it can be used in any tax jurisdiction that accepts the FIFO and LIFO tax standards. FIFO stands for first in first out and LIFO looks at last in first out treatment of your holdings. This tax filer system either imports a CSV file from your crypto exchange containing all of the year's transactions or uses an API import tool that allows your transaction information held on the exchange to connect with the CryptoTrader software.

Over three dozen exchanges are supported by CryptoTrader. The tax software spits out various short-term and long-term sales reports, appropriate tax forms, an end-of-year positions report and a TurboTax online direct import file. The platform also allows a tax accountant to import, review and file tax reports on your behalf.

A Hobbyist plan is $49 per tax season and covers up to 100 trades. For the novice trader, the Day Trader plan is $99 and allows up to 1500 trades per year. The platform also provides free access to a limited version of the software that could be used to just calculate your tax obligations.

Overall, this platform has an intuitive interface that makes the program easy to use and novice friendly. On the downside, the platform does focus primarily on the US market and IRS forms. It also has a limited number of exchanges that are currently supported.

2. Bear.tax

This software platform also allows you to quickly compute and file tax reports. It too focuses on the US market. You'll either import your trades via an API integration or by uploading a CSV file. Tax documents are auto generated for you. It also has the ability to calculate taxes for more unusual transactions like, gifts, staking rewards, airdrops, hard forks, referrals, mining, voting rewards, community rewards, inheritances, crypto payments and earning programs.

This tax option has more clout as it supports more taxable situations than the CryptoTrader platform. For hodlers, Bear has you covered with a transaction review function, which allows you to search specific transactions and make modifications. This ensures that you input the correct cost basis for a specific time or date. A key feature is that the Bear platform offers historical pricing data for every supported cryptocurrency making it much easier to assess market values.

This tax software also supports high-frequency traders and BOTS. So, if you've used bots like 3Commas to help automate your trading, this software supports those types of transactions. Bear supports over 50 exchanges.

A Basic plan of $10 per tax year gives you up to 20 transactions. The Intermediate plan of $45 bumps up the transactions to 200. And the $85 Expert plan allows up to 1000 transactions. This tax platform is one of the most economical ones in the market.

3. CoinTracking.com

This software not only calculates tax liabilities, but it also tracks your transactions producing real-time profit-loss reports. You'll have access to a myriad of reports and tools like a personal portfolio analysis, trade imports, tax declarations, coin charts and coin trends.

CoinTracking is one of the most popular in the marketplace with over 610,000 active users and over 750 CPAs and corporate clients. It supports over 7500 coins with historical data going back a decade. This platform is suitable for novice investors, traders and businesses. You'll be able to generate a number of reports for profit and losses, as well as realized and unrealized gains. Over 70 exchanges are supported by CoinTracking. It also provides you with the option of importing data from cold storage devices like Ledger and Trezor. Both API integration and direct blockchain network synch is available.

Unlike CryptoTrader and Bear, CoinTracking has 12 tax treatment methods you can use, making it more compatible with more tax jurisdictions than the other two. If you're living outside of the US, then this is a good option to consider. The software also has the advantage of being able to find missing and duplicate transactions, thus making it easier come tax time.

The Free option supports up to 200 transactions with limited features. With all of the bells and whistles the software comes with, you should try before you buy to see if this powerhouse is what you need. The Pro Plan is $10.99 per month or $131.88 per year and can track up to 3500 transactions. If you've only made a few trades over the course of a year, consider using one of the other cheaper options like Bear.tax.

4. Koinly.com

This software platform is the most versatile in that it directly supports more than 20 countries and their tax systems. The US, Canada, Australia, New Zealand, many European Union countries and a few Asian countries are currently being supported by Koinly. The platform was developed in close collaboration with local tax firms to ensure it complies with all the applicable tax laws.

The portfolio analysis tool gives great insights into how your holdings are doing in terms of returns, profit and loss calculations and capital gains. Koinly makes it easy for importing and exporting transaction data from several exchanges using the API integration app. Data from margin trading, futures trading, staking, lending and defi can also be imported.

Your tax documents are autogenerated by Koinly and can be previewed freely. They make it convenient for you to download your capital gains in a format that can be easily imported into online tax filing software like TurboTax, TaxAct, Drake, and H&R Block. As with CoinTracking, this platform also enables you to quickly locate missing or duplicate transactions. It also has a smart matching system to makes sure you don't make any tax overpayments. Koinly supports over 350 crypto exchanges, 50 wallets and 6000 different cryptocurrencies. This software platform has the best tax support of any tax software currently out in the market.

The Free plan provides support for up to 10,000 transactions and 50 exchanges. Unfortunately, it won't generate the necessary tax reports for the country you're residing in, nor will you be able to export to TurboTax. You'll need to invest in a paid plan if you want to file those forms automatically. The basic Hodler plan is set at $49 and is ideal for novice and intermediate investors who have under 100 transactions per year and want to simplify tax reporting requirements. The Trader plan at $99 allows for greater flexibility with up to 1000 transactions being recorded, which makes it ideal for novice traders. And the $179 Trader / Pro account kicks it up to 3000 transactions per year.

Do-It-Yourself Capital Gains Calculations:

Should you prefer tracking your investment gains and losses yourself, you'll need some basic information that all major exchanges provide and keep track of. To calculate the capital gains owing on a typical long-term crypto investment, you'll need to record the following information on your tax return:

- Transaction date as to when you purchased the cryptocurrency.
- Initial amount paid for the coin being sold.
- Disposition date as to when you cashed in your holding.
- Final amount received when you sold the coin.
- Transaction fees assessed to purchase and dispose of the coin.

Once you have this basic information, you'll need to first calculate the initial adjusted cost basis of your purchase. In a simplified example, this is accomplished by subtracting your initial transaction fees paid from the cost of your initial purchase. If you're disposing of multiple purchase transactions at the same time, then you'll need to determine the average cost less the fees associated with these transactions. This calculation gives you your adjusted cost basis.

Your capital gains owing is based on the amount you sold your coin for, less your adjusted cost basis and any transaction fees associated with the sale. This calculation determines what your gains or losses are for the disposition. If the disposition falls under the category of being capital gains, then the long-term capital gains tax rates in the US are 0 percent, 15 percent and 20 percent, depending on your income.

If you're in Canada, the capital gains tax rate is based on 50 percent of the gain or loss. You'll pay income tax on half of the gains you've made.

How to Lower Your Tax Obligations?

Keeping the five factors previously discussed front of mind that the taxman will use to determine if you are engaged in a business activity with your cryptos or not, is an important proactive step.

Some additional factors to consider for lowering your tax obligations are some of the following:

1. Timing the Sale of Your Holdings.

Apply the same general rules for exiting crypto positions as you would stocks. Hold them for at least one year before selling. You're less likely to run into capital gain challenges.

Next, assess whether or not postponing a taxable event like cashing out coins, trading coins, or buying goods and services with cryptos can be moved to the next tax year. For example, if its December and you're considering selling a portion of your holdings, could you hold off doing so until the next taxation year. The worst-case scenario is that even if you trigger a taxable event at least it'll occur in the following year, giving you ample time to prepare for that tax liability.

Depending on the tax jurisdiction you're living in, you could also consider cashing out 1/2 of your position in the current tax year and by waiting several weeks cash out the balance in the following tax year. This enables you to split your taxable gains between the two years. If you live in the US, take a look at the capital gains crypto tax calculator found at Nerdwallet.com (https://www.nerdwallet.com/article/taxes/capital-gains-tax-rates).

2. Re-entering a Position too Soon.

Should you incur a capital loss for a particular holding, avoid re-entering the same crypto until at least 30 days after your last sale. Otherwise, you may not benefit from claiming that capital loss. With the crypto market being so volatile, this scenario could pop up should a great buy-in opportunity be presenting itself. Just keep in mind the potential tax implications of popping back into the market too quickly.

3. Becoming a Crypto Entrepreneur.

Another option to consider is looking into the possibility of becoming a freelancer or starting a business. Some of those crypto gains could be written down by claiming certain business expenses that'll reduce your overall taxable income and liability. When you're a freelancer or run a business almost everything is tax deductible as it relates to earning an income. Be sure to check this option out with the help of a tax advisor before jumping in with both feet.

4. Moving to a Tax Haven.

As a last resort, if you feel that you don't want to pay taxes on any gains generated, you do have the remote option of moving to a country that currently doesn't tax crypto gains. I should emphasize the word "currently" as tax regulations can change in a country you're considering moving to. Also, the biggest challenge is getting the necessary visas. Moving to a tax haven is just not a practical option for most crypto investors.

Some of the countries that don't currently tax crypto gains are:

- United Arab Emirates - no capital gains nor income taxes but it has a high cost of living.
- Switzerland - if you're a professional crypto trader, you might qualify for a visa.
- Germany - no taxes are paid on crypto transactions if held longer

than 1 year.
- Portugal - no taxes. Hard to relocate to if you're not a European citizen.
- Belarus - no taxation of crypto profits until 2023.
- Malta - like Germany, it levies no crypto taxes on positions held longer than 1 year. However, non-Europeans are taxed a minimum of 15,000 Euros.
- Singapore - no taxes on gains as long as you're not a day trader. The downside is that you need to be a high-income earner in order to relocate here.
- Malaysia - has the same criteria as Singapore.
- Hong Kong - like Germany, you won't pay taxes on gains held longer than 1 year.
- Puerto Rico - great for US citizens. Any gains made after becoming a citizen are tax exempt. This applies to any holdings you have made prior to moving there and establishing your permanent residence.

∾

CLOSING REMARKS

By now you should have a better feel as to what the cryptocurrency market has to offer. If you're as excited as I am, you're already taking action in getting things set up so that you can tap into the incredible wealth potential that cryptocurrency investing has to offer. Being early into this new asset class makes it easier to realize substantial gains from even small positions.

As I've mentioned throughout the book, investing directly in cryptocurrencies is only one approach to getting exposure to this growing asset class. You also have the wealth generation potential of the stock market to help you. Companies investing in blockchain technology, ETF's, and options trading are all gearing up to take advantage of the enormous wealth generation potential of cryptocurrencies.

www.ingramcontent.com/pod-product-compliance
Lightning Source LLC
Chambersburg PA
CBHW081811200326
41597CB00023B/4229